MATH
PROJECTS FOR YOUNG SCIENTISTS

DAVID A. THOMAS

MATH PROJECTS FOR YOUNG SCIENTISTS

PROJECTS FOR YOUNG SCIENTISTS
FRANKLIN WATTS I 1988
NEW YORK I LONDON I TORONTO I SYDNEY

In writing this book, the author was greatly influenced by
*A Guide to Establishing a Science/Mathematics Research Program
in High School*, by Goodman, Harvey, and others, published in
1982 by the New York City Board of Education. ED244810.

Diagrams by Vantage Art, Inc.
Photographs courtesy of: UPI/Bettmann Newsphotos: p. 15;
Westinghouse: p. 17; Leonard Lee Rue III/Photo Researchers: p. 43
(top); Henry Rasof: pp. 43 (bottom), 44 (bottom), 76, 82
(bottom), 83, 93, 94 (top), 95; Hugh Spencer/Photo Researchers:
p. 44 (top left); Walter Dawn/Photo Researchers: p. 44 (top
right); Art Resource: p. 51, 78; David Scharf/Peter Arnold:
p. 79; Colin G. Butler/Photo Researchers: p. 80; Mary M. Thacher/
Photo Researchers: p. 82 (top); Ray Ellis/Photo Researchers: p. 85;
Deneb Robotics Inc.: p. 91; Richard B. Hait/Photo Researchers:
p. 94 (bottom); Russ Kinne/Photo Researchers: p. 97 (top); Lynn
McLaren/Photo Researchers: p. 97 (bottom); Artmatrix: pp. 98, 110, 115;
Benoit Mandelbrot: p. 116

Library of Congress Cataloging-in-Publication Data

Thomas, David A. (David Allen), 1946-
Math projects for young scientists.

(Projects for young scientists)
Bibliography: p.
Includes index.
Summary: Suggests topics and tips on preparing a project or original
research in pure mathematics for a science fair. Discusses such areas
as probability, geometry, topology, number theory, and sequences.
1. Mathematics—Study and teaching—Juvenile literature. (1. Mathematics
—Problems, exercises, etc. 2. Mathematical recreations) I. Title. II. Series.
QA11.T62 1988   510   87-21064
ISBN 0-531-10523-7

Copy 1

TO MY DAD

CONTENTS

MATH
PROJECTS FOR YOUNG SCIENTISTS

1

A MATH PROJECT
FOR YOU

Do you dream of a career in mathematics, computer science, engineering, physics, or astronomy? Can you imagine yourself making scientific discoveries, designing new cars or spaceships, or listening to the stars with a radio telescope? If your answer is yes, you can start today to make your dream a reality by renewing your interest in mathematics, the language of science and engineering.

By its very nature, an education in mathematics should never be taken for granted. Warming a seat in a math class may get you a grade, but if you are serious about a career in mathematics, engineering, or the sciences, your study of mathematics should become more personal. One of the most popular ways to do this is via a student research project.

Most student research projects in mathematics are conducted to satisfy course requirements or for extra credit. Work on such projects typically extends over a period of several weeks and involves both library work and problem solving or model building. Frequently, when the projects are finished, they are presented in class and/or displayed during parent-teacher conferences.

The other main reason that students do mathematics projects is to enter science fairs. In recent years, math projects have been among the top award winners in national competitions. But whether your research project is to be presented at school or a science fair, don't let the word "research" scare you. Remember, you're not trying to rival NASA's space program! You can investigate many topics without knowing college-level mathematics.

PURE AND APPLIED MATH

Most of the project ideas in this book deal with "pure" mathematics, as opposed to "applied" mathematics. Pure mathematics deals with concepts and techniques built only upon mathematical concerns. Applied mathematics transfers mathematical concepts and techniques to other disciplines, such as physics.

Both pure and applied mathematics offer excellent opportunities for student research. However, research in applied mathematics often requires a background in both mathematics and the discipline to which it is applied. For instance, if you have taken physics, perhaps a problem in applied mathematics is appropriate for you. On the other hand, if you have no background in physics or any other discipline to which mathematics might be "applied," you need a topic with few "prerequisites." Most of the topics suggested in this book are of just such a nature. You can "get into" them quickly.

THE PEDIGREE OF
A GOOD PROJECT

What do teachers and science fair judges look for in a research project? Since most science fair exhibits are attractive, well documented, and interesting, what additional quality or qualities do the judges search for as they review the entries and select the winners? Of all the features which could be mentioned, one stands out as most important: originality.

Originality in mathematics can be exhibited in many ways. Every new discovery is "an original" and requires genuine creativity. For instance, you might discover a new **theorem,** a mathematical "law" or principle, in geometry. By being the first person to state and prove the theorem, you demonstrate originality.

Originality is also exhibited whenever a person finds a new way to solve an old problem. No new theorems may emerge from the work, but new insights are revealed nonetheless. Such originality may take the form of a new proof of an old theorem, the use of some existing problem-solving technique in a new context, or even an original way of understanding and stating a familiar problem. In other words, a project may exhibit originality of approach rather than originality of results.

As you can see, creativity and originality in mathematics is a broad enough concept that you need not be anxious that somebody else might have already investigated your mathematics topic. It matters little whether your topic is new or old as long as a flash of *your* insight can be clearly seen. It is the quality of this original thinking, rather than the depth or complexity of your topic, that is most important to your teacher and to science fair judges.

IMPROVING YOUR ORIGINALITY QUOTIENT

Is there anything you can do to improve your "originality quotient"? One way is to be more *problem-oriented* than *solution-oriented*. Learn to turn problems over in your mind, identifying facts, observing relationships, clarifying the question. Try to restate the problem in your own words, represent it in some different manner, or see it in some different light. It is this type of mental activity that sows the seeds of genuine insight, revealing previously unseen relationships.

It has been said that Albert Einstein's great strength lay in his ability to hold a problem in his mind for days, weeks, even months while he slowly studied its features. He said himself that he understood things very, very slowly. Such a mind is like "a glacier, moving slowly yet ultimately changing the landscape of human history."

HIGH SCHOOL "ORIGINALS"

Fortunately, great thinking among students is not a thing of the past. Here is a list of a few of the mathematics projects which have won major awards in the past few years in the Westinghouse Science Talent Search.

1983	First place	Paul Chinh Ning studied functions of the positive integers.
	Second place	Michael I. Hyman developed software and hardware for three-dimensional graphics on a microcomputer.
	Finalist	Janet Lin Pan examined the divisibility of sums of powers of integers.

PAUL NING (CENTER), MICHAEL HYMAN (LEFT), AND ERIC KOIDE (RIGHT)— 1983 WINNERS IN THE WESTINGHOUSE SCIENCE TALENT SEARCH. NING AND HYMAN HAD MATH PROJECTS.

1984	Third place	Michael Tai-Lin wrote a computer program to solve Rubik's cube from all possible starting positions.
1985	First place	Alan John Hu devised a method to speed the location of information on a computer disk.
	Third place	Michael Friedman used his computer to investigate odd perfect numbers.
1986	First place	Wei Jing Zhu extended a famous mathematical problem to include complex numbers.
	Sixth place	Jessica L. Boklan found a way to generate all reversible products for two to four digits.
1987	Second place	Elizabeth Lee Wilmer worked on the three-color map problem: What kinds of maps are colorable using only three colors so that no two countries sharing a common border are the same color?
	Fifth place	Daniel Julius Bernstein discovered improved ways to compute the values of certain numbers, such as pi and *e*, the base of the natural logarithms.

**ELIZABETH WILMER PLACED SECOND
IN THE 1987 WESTINGHOUSE
CONTEST WITH HER MATH PROJECT.**

These students are all winners partially because their projects exhibited originality and insight. But they also chose topics appropriate to their interests and abilities, then put a lot of themselves into their projects.

SELECTING A TOPIC
RIGHT FOR YOU—
THE PROCESS

The following principles should guide you in selecting a topic. First, choose something that genuinely interests you. Second, take advantage of every opportunity to broaden your exposure to mathematics. There is much more to mathematics than the typical junior or senior high school can offer. Third, select a topic in a branch of mathematics that is somewhat familiar. For example, if you have had a brief introduction to probability, consider developing your interest in that area. Fourth, seek the help and guidance of mathematics teachers who know you well enough to help you select a topic appropriate to your abilities and background.

After you have narrowed your search for a topic to a particular branch of mathematics, you must pose your research problem "operationally" so that you will know when it has been completed. One reference that you might find helpful at this point is the book *The Art of Problem Posing* by Stephen Brown and Marion Walter (Philadelphia: The Franklin Institute Press, 1983).

GENERAL AREAS
OF RESEARCH

Many different areas of mathematics provide excellent opportunities for research. Several of these areas are relatively easy to "get into" and do not assume that you have taken college-level mathematics courses. Five such areas are listed below along with a few references which you can use as starting points in your library search.

For sample project ideas in each area, turn to the chapter in this book identified in the parentheses.

1. Combinatorics and Probability (Chapter 3)

How many different ways can a set of objects be arranged? What is the probability that a given event will take place? This branch of mathematics is one of the easier to "get into." It deals with such topics as combinations, permutations, tree diagrams, probability, and Pascal's triangle.

Reference

Niven, I. *Mathematics of Choice*. Washington: Mathematical Association of America, 1975.

2. Fibonacci and Lucas Numbers (Chapter 4)

Famous number sequences that appear in seemingly unrelated mathematical topics and in nature. Includes such topics as the golden section, the Binet formula, and the genealogy of a worker bee.

References

Bicknell, M., and Hoggatt, J.E., Jr. (eds.). *Fibonacci's Problem Book*. San Jose, Calif.: San Jose University, Fibonacci Association, 1974.

Hoggatt, V.E. *Fibonacci and Lucas Numbers*. Boston: Houghton Mifflin, 1969.

Huntley, H.E. *The Divine Proportion*. New York: Dover, 1970.

Posamentier, Alfred S. *Excursions in Advanced Euclidean Geometry*. Menlo Park, Calif.: Addison-Wesley, 1984.

3. Number Theory (Chapter 5)

A study of the many unusual and interesting features of numbers, including divisibility tests in various systems of numeration, Wilson's theorem, magic squares, and Diophantine equations.

References

Dudley, U. *Elementary Number Theory.* San Francisco: W.H. Freeman, 1978.

Hardy, G.H., and Wright, E.M. *Introduction to the Theory of Numbers.* Oxford: Oxford University Press, 1980.

Sierpinski, W. *250 Problems in Elementary Number Theory.* New York: Elsevier, 1970.

4. Sequences and Series (Chapter 6)

Arithmetic and geometric sequences are common. Extensions of these topics include arithmetic, geometric, harmonic, and finite series, and convergence of infinite series.

References

Hall, H.S., and Knight, S.R. *Higher Algebra.* London: Macmillan, 1957.

Knopp, K. *Infinite Sequences and Series.* New York: Dover, 1956.

Among the many methods used in the investigation of sequences and series, perhaps the most common method of proof is **mathematical induction.** A few references for this technique are provided below.

References

Polya, G. *Induction and Analogy in Mathematics.* Princeton, N.J.: Princeton University Press, 1954.

Shklarsky, D.O., and Chenstov, N.M. *Selected Problems and Theorems in Elementary Mathematics.* Moscow: Mir Publishers, 1979.

5. Geometry and Topology (Chapter 7)

Take an activity-oriented approach to geometry, covering such topics as translations, rotations, reflections, dilation, and projections.

References
Yaglom, I.M. *Geometric Transformations.* Vols. 1–3. Washington: Mathematical Association of America, 1975, 1979.

Coxeter, H.S., and Greitzer, S. *Geometry Revisited.* Washington: Mathematical Association of America, 1975.

Modenov, P.S., and Parkhomenko, A.S. *Geometric Transformations.* New York: Academic Press, 1965.

6. Dynamical Systems, Julia Sets, and Fractals (Chapter 9)

References
Blanchard, Paul. *Complex Analytic Dynamics on the Riemann Sphere.* Minneapolis: Institute for Mathematics and Its Applications, University of Minnesota, 1984.

Devaney, Robert L. *An Introduction to Chaotic Dynamical Systems.* Menlo Park, Calif.: Benjamin/Cummings, 1986.

Dewdney, A.K. "Computer Recreations." *Scientific American,* August 1985.

Mandelbrot, Benoit. *The Fractal Geometry of Nature.* San Francisco: W.H. Freeman, 1982.

Peitgen, H.O., and Richter, P.H. *The Beauty of Fractals.*
New York: Springer-Verlag, 1986.

Peitgen, H.O.; Saupe, D.; and von Haeseler, F. "Cayley's
Problem and Julia Sets." *The Mathematical Intelligencer,*
vol. 6, no. 2.

PROJECT TITLES

Knowing what other students have chosen as projects
may make your choice easier by suggesting possibilities.
The following lists of titles represent a very small sample
of mathematics projects presented in the past at
science fairs and science searches. The projects listed
here were not all winners, so don't draw conclusions from
the titles. Simply review the list as a sample of student
interests. For a more comprehensive list of titles, consult
the *Mathematics Project Handbook* by Adrian Hess, Res-
ton, Va.: (NCTM, 1982).

Algebra, Game Theory, and Number Theory

- New approach to Quadratic Equations
- An Investigation of the Twin Primes Problem
- Divisibility
- Polyominoes
- Comparison of Loops and Groups
- The Function $x^y = y^x$
- Theory of Braids
- Finite Sums of Polynomials
- Diophantine Equations via Continued Fractions

Analysis

- Convex Smooth Curves
- Minimal Surface Area Experiments with Soap Films
- Arc Length
- A New Method of Summing Certain Infinite Series

- Orbital Calculus
- Curvature of Droplets
- Logical Analysis of Infinity and Infinite Set Theory

Arithmetic
- Binary Counter
- Binary Logarithms
- Systems of Large Numbers
- The Duodecimal System
- The Ancient Quipu
- A Number System to an Irrational Base
- Computation in Systems Other Than Decimal

Geometry
- Biangular System of Coordinates
- Finding the Area of an Ellipse
- The Triangle Theorem of Desargues
- Golden Section
- An Extension of the Theorem of Pythagoras
- Quadratic Surfaces
- Folding Polyhedrons
- Pyramids
- The Quartic Curves

Statistics and Probability
- A Vector Approach to Statistics
- Mathematics and Games of Chance
- Determination of Pi by Probability
- Geometric Figures in Probability
- The Number *e* by Spinning a Needle

Topology
- Map Coloring
- One-Sided Surfaces
- Topology of Knots
- "Rubber Geometry"—Some Properties of Topological Surfaces

RESOURCES

By making use of local and national resources, you can improve the odds that you will make a good choice when selecting a topic for your research. A number of useful resources are discussed below.

1. If your school has a mathematics club, join it and start attending the meetings. You will encounter topics not covered in class and meet people who share your interest in research.
2. Invite guest speakers to your school. As you listen to them talk about their research, you will begin to understand the research process better yourself.
3. The National Science Foundation sponsors summer institutes for high school students interested in mathematics and science. Check with your science and math teachers and counselors or write the National Science Foundation, Washington, DC 20550.
4. Most states have a local Academy of Science or Junior Academy of Science. The Mathematics Department at the nearest public university can help you contact these organizations.
5. Use the resources of your nearest university library.

2

RESEARCHING AND PRESENTING YOUR PROJECT

Once you have identified a topic for your research, your next stop should be the library. Using all available resources, read everything you can on your chosen topic. Since most high school libraries are not set up to support research in mathematics, you will probably need to visit a college or university library.

When you get to the library, go immediately to the reference desk. The reference librarian is a specialist in locating information and can save you hours of searching. College libraries store information in many forms not found in most high school libraries (microfilm, microfiche, computer databases, government bulletins and pamphlet files, etc.). Without the help of a librarian, there is a good chance that you will not find some of the resources available to you.

WHY REVIEW
THE LITERATURE?

When doing library research for a science project, a person normally does not use references older than about ten years. Science changes so fast that information becomes outdated quickly. This is not the case in mathematics. Textbooks and journal articles take decades to become obsolete. For this reason, when searching through card catalogs, indices to periodical literature, and other resources, you will need to take older publications into account.

Another important difference between library research in mathematics and the sciences arises over the issue of scholarly authority. In science, a researcher may justify certain of his or her decisions (choice of experimental design, equipment, statistical tests, etc.) by citing well-known scientists who have supported such decisions in the past. In such cases, where the power of logic alone is not enough to recommend a particular action, the opinions of recognized experts are used as guidelines. This is rarely the case in mathematics.

In mathematics, the only acceptable reason for any decision is solid logic. Insight may provide a new perspective, but logic must then justify the perspective.

For this reason, students doing research in mathematics may or may not cite outside authorities in their final reports. In the case of mathematical research, the primary purpose of the review of literature is to provide background information for the researcher. This background information provides the researcher with basic concepts and vocabulary, valuable insights, and skills—all of which may be critical in the research.

SOLVING YOUR PROBLEM

It is not possible for this or any other book to tell you how to solve the problem you have chosen to research. Even the background reading that you do may not readily suggest which strategy you ought to pursue. There is another field of study, however, which might provide just the insight that you need.

The study of general problem-solving techniques is

called **heuristics.** By learning a variety of general mathematical problem-solving strategies, you equip yourself to be a better problem solver in general and in your research in particular. What are some of these general problem-solving strategies?

1. *Characterize the problem.* What is given? What is needed? What is missing? What are you looking for? Are any unnecessary data given? Look at several examples. Do any special cases limit the range of possible answers? Can you simplify the problem exploiting symmetry or "without loss of generality" arguments, where the entire problem is reduced to considering a special case?

2. *Have you seen this before?* Or, have you seen this problem in a slightly different form? If so, can you transfer to the current problem any part of the method used to solve the previous problem? Construct a similar problem with fewer variables and solve it. By "relaxing" one or more of the conditions, can you learn anything about the original problem?

3. *Look for a pattern.* By examining the overall features of the series $1 + 2 + \ldots + 100$, young Frederick Gauss recognized a pattern: $1 + 100 = 2 + 99 = 3 + 98 = \ldots 101$. This insight led immediately to the observation that fifty such pairs could be formed. The problem of finding the sum of the integers from 1 to 100 then became a simple multiplication task, $50 \times 101 = 5{,}050$.

4. *Simplification.* Sometimes a relatively simple underlying relationship or pattern is obscured by "messy" quantities and expressions. Try substituting simple symbols for the messy ones; then look for an underlying relationship. Regrouping terms in a complicated expression may accomplish the same end.

5. *Reduction.* Can your problem be broken up into smaller, more manageable subproblems?
6. *Work backward.* When trying to prove a theorem that you know to be true, it may be revealing to begin at the conclusion and backtrack logically.
7. *Make a list.* If you have access to a computer, it may be possible to make an exhaustive list of all the possible outcomes of some process. If you are interested in specific outcomes of that process, they should be included in your exhaustive list.
8. *Simulation and modeling.* A mathematical model may be developed which imitates some complicated process in mathematics or in the real world If the results obtained using the simulation are accurate, then the simulation is a success.
9. *Formal logic.* Mathematical induction is a powerful tool in many areas of mathematics. So also is the technique called "indirect proof," also known as proof by contradiction.
10. *Does your answer make sense?* Check your answer using common sense and alternative reasoning.

Finally, whenever you try to solve a problem look for several ways to represent its features: make and label a drawing, make a list of features, write an equation expressing relationships, etc. The more ways that you can represent the problem, the more likely you are to discover the hidden relationships that are the key to the solution.

THE FORM OF
YOUR FINAL REPORT

If you plan to present your project at school, your teacher may specify the form of your report. If no form is specified or if you plan to enter your project in a science fair, your final report should include the following:

1. A descriptive title.
2. An abstract of the project (200–300 words).
3. A discussion of the problem under investigation. This provides a context for your research and findings.
4. An operationally stated problem statement. This serves to focus your research.
5. A discussion of your methods, findings, and conclusions.
6. Possible directions for further research on this topic, unanswered questions, etc.
7. Appendix items (tables, charts, etc.).
8. Bibliography.

Report writing in mathematics is especially difficult because the writing must clearly trace the thread of logic running through an argument which frequently shifts from one medium of expression to another. For instance, a typical report might begin with a paragraph of textual discussion, shift to a series of equations, return to the textual approach, then make use of a diagram, etc. Under such conditions it can be difficult to draw the "thread" in clearly.

One resource that may be of help is the book *How to Write Mathematics* (Providence, R.I.: American Mathematical Society, 1973). Paul Halmos's article is probably the most useful in this book.

PLANNING YOUR EXHIBIT—GETTING THE MESSAGE ACROSS

The purpose of your exhibit is to tell the story of your research project clearly and accurately. In order to succeed in this purpose you need to design your exhibit with certain principles in mind.

1. Your exhibit must *clearly* focus on the problem that you studied and the originality that you demonstrated. The degree to which you succeed in *visually* highlighting the originality of your thinking will play a role in impressing your teacher and the science fair judges.
2. The overall layout of the display should create a clear center of interest. In that center of interest you should present the focus or message of your exhibit.
3. The other parts of the exhibit should complement and support the center of interest without cluttering up the display.
4. Lettering should be done in ink or with transfer letters. Remember, clear thinking impresses teachers and judges—not big words.
5. Your complete report and other supporting documents may be displayed in a notebook.
6. Any models or equipment in the display should be clearly labeled both in terms of what they are and how they were used in the investigation.

PLANNING YOUR EXHIBIT—IMPORTANT PRACTICAL CONSIDERATIONS

Whether you plan to exhibit your project at school or a science fair, there will be practical limitations to the amount of space you can use. Your teacher can tell you how much space is available at school. If you plan to enter a science fair, *before* you begin to build your display, obtain a copy of the "Instructions for Exhibitors" and read them very carefully. Pay special attention to the materials and services which will or will not be available at each exhibit: Is a table provided? What about electricity?

Many fairs have adopted the following maximum display sizes of the International Science and Engineering Fair (ISEF): 48 inches wide and 30 inches deep. If you keep your exhibit within these limitations, you can probably enter it in most science fairs in this country.

WHICH WAY TO
THE SCIENCE FAIR?

There are hundreds of science fairs in the United States every year. Most states have regional fairs which are routinely advertised through professional associations, newspapers, and other means. To locate a fair close to home, start by asking your science and math teachers.

If your school district does not have a science fair planned, information about regional fairs may be obtained from the National Science Teachers Association, 1742 Connecticut Avenue NW, Washington, DC 20009. Or, you may write Science Service, 1719 N Street NW, Washington, DC 20036.

Another excellent resource is *Winning with Science: The Complete Guide to Science Research and Programs for Students* by William S. Loiry (Sarasota, Fla.: Loiry Publishing House, 1983).

NATIONAL COMPETITIONS

Several science fairs and science competitions conducted at the national rather than the local or state levels accept mathematics projects as entries. These competitions are for serious students of science and mathematics. A few of the better-known national competitions are listed on the next page:

- *Westinghouse Science Talent Search.* This is a science research-paper competition open to high school seniors. Students submit a 1,000-word report of their research activities and findings. The deadline for entry is December 15 of each year. For information and an application packet, write to Science Service at the address listed above.

- *National Student Science Competition.* This competition is a program of the National Consortium for Black Professional Development. For more information, write to The National Consortium For Black Professional Development, 1359 South 3rd Street, Louisville, KY 40208.

- *International Science and Engineering Fair.* Winners from state and local Science and Engineering Fairs are invited to participate. Students in the ninth to twelfth grades take part. For more information, write to Science Service at the address listed above.

3

COMBINATORICS AND PROBABILITY

In some table games, each move is determined by a random event, like the roll of a die or the spin of a wheel. Knowing something about the probable outcomes of such events can make you a better game player.

In the real "game" of life, random events and forces sometimes play important roles, either providing opportunity or bringing disaster. In life, knowing something about the likelihood of both opportunity and disaster can help you make better decisions and preparations.

Mathematicians study random events for several reasons. First, understanding random behavior or events helps to evaluate the magnitude of a potential threat or opportunity. For example, if the probability of a tornado flattening your home is very small, why worry? On the other hand, if the probability is high, start planning to survive both physically and economically! All insurance premiums are based on just this type of consideration.

A second reason for studying random behavior and events is that it can help you understand important natural and artificial processes. For example, an understanding of the apparently random behavior of cars on a freeway can lead to an understanding of the most important features of freeway design. You see, in order to recognize intentional or structured behavior, you must first know what random behavior looks like. That is, you have to know the difference.

The study of combinatorics and probability is the study of possibilities and random events. The topics in this chapter will introduce you to a few of the features of this important branch of mathematics.

GETTING STARTED

An introduction to the study of **combinatorics** usually involves questions of the following type: How many different ways can eight people be seated around a table? What is the most efficient format for car license plates in a state having one million vehicles on the road? How many different results could you get when you flip thirteen coins?

An introduction to the study of **probability** frequently addresses questions of a similar type: What is the probability that, in randomly seating four married couples around a table, each man will be seated beside his wife? What is the probability that your car license plate will contain at least three integers in consecutive order? What is the probability that in flipping thirteen coins, exactly seven will land heads up?

As you can see, combinatorics and probability often are used to address similar problem situations. If your choose to investigate a topic involving either of these branches of mathematics, look under both headings in the library card catalog. This will increase the probability that you will find the information you need.

The problems found in this chapter vary in difficulty and barely begin to illustrate the research possibilities in combinatorics and probability. Some of the problems have been solved by other mathematicians; others have not. Some problems may be solved quickly and should be expanded into a topic suitable for a class project. Other problems may be complex enough to occupy your interest for some time and form the basis of a science fair project. If you find an idea interesting, check with your teacher concerning its level of difficulty. And with respect to the matter of originality, remember that it is enough to show originality of method. Originality of results is not required.

FOR CHESS PLAYERS

Project 1
Determine the
(a) smallest number of bishops needed to control every unoccupied square on the board.
(b) smallest number of kings required to control every unoccupied square on the board.
(c) greatest number of knights that can be used so that no knight lies on a square controlled by another.
(d) number of different ways that a single board may be set up using a single set of chessmen.

If you have never played chess, this problem may seem foreign. However, with the following information, you should make some progress:

- A chessboard is an 8 × 8 array of squares.
- A bishop controls all squares on the diagonals on which it lies up to and including the first square occupied by another piece.
- A king controls all squares adjacent to the square where it is located.
- A knight controls all squares which are at a distance of one vertical or horizontal square *plus* one diagonal square from its location.

HOW MANY WAYS
CAN THIS BE DONE?

Project 2

Imagine a regular pentagon: five equal sides, five equal angles. Starting at one of the vertices (corners), draw a diagonal line to each of the other vertices. The diagonals **partition** (divide) the pentagon into three triangles. How many *different* ways can this be done to the pentagon using nonintersecting diagonals?

Repeat this process with several other convex (no "dents") polygons, each time noting the number of different partitions possible. Continue this process looking for a pattern.

Try to find a formula for calculating the number of different ways that a convex polygon can be decomposed into triangles using nonintersecting diagonals within the polygon.

Project 3

Imagine that three-dimensional space comes equipped with a grid system. The lines of the grid are like the lines on graph paper. Each point in the grid is formed by the intersection of three perpendicular grid lines. Starting at any point, travel to another point by following the grid lines. Do not "cut across" diagonally from one point or line to another.

You could follow a lot of routes in moving from one point to another. Some routes are longer than others. The shortest distance between any two points will lie along one or more shortest paths.

See if you can determine if the number of shortest paths along grid lines is related to the points selected or any feature of their relative positions in the grid.

Project 4

A 2 × 2 rectangle is to be covered with 1 × 2 and 2 × 2 bricks. You may use any combintion of bricks as long as the rectangle is covered exactly and no bricks are "trimmed" to fit. How many ways can this be done?

What if the rectangle is 2 × 3? 2 × 4? 2 × 5? Determine the number of different ways that this can be done (a) on a 2 × N rectangle, (b) on a 3 × N rectangle, (c) on a 4 × N rectangle, (d) on an M × N rectangle.

Project 5

Suppose that the United Nations decided to create a library of translation dictionaries: English to German and German to English; English to Japanese and Japanese to English, . . .

Determine the number of dictionaries needed to translate between any two of the languages used for communication if there are (a) ten languages in use, (b) twenty languages in use, (c) twenty-five languages in use, (d) etc.

Determine the number of translators needed if each could speak at most (a) three languages, (b) four languages, (c) five languages, (d) etc.

Project 6

A school day has seven periods at a certain high school. Tenth-grade English, social studies, study hall, and physical education are offered every period. Tenth-grade math and science are offered three periods during the day, overlapping one period. A student wants to take each of the above-listed courses plus a shop course.

Determine the number of different schedules possible for the student if the shop course meets (a) once during the day, (b) twice during the day, (c) every period.

Project 7

There are 300 parking spaces in the student parking lot at a certain high school. On a typical day, 175 students drive cars to school and park at random locations in the lot.

Determine the number of different ways the cars can be parked in the lot. Determine the probability of two or more specific cars parking side by side on any day. For two consecutive days. For three consecutive days. For n days.

Project 8

A panel discussion is planned for a student council. The panel consists of four males and four females, one from each of the four high school classes (grades 9–12). The panel will sit at a round table with the moderator, Mr. Jones.

Determine

(a) the number of different ways that the nine people can be seated.
(b) the probability that the representatives from each class will be seated beside one another if random seating is used.
(c) the probability that no two representatives of the same class will be seated beside one another.

MISCELLANEOUS

The following problems invite a variety of approaches.

Project 9

Prove that in any group of people, at least two have the same number of friends in the group.

Project 10

Prove that, in a gathering of six individuals, there are either three who are mutual acquaintances or three who are strangers to one another.

Project 11

A table tennis champion decides to play at least one match a day over a period of two weeks, playing in all no more than twenty matches.

Prove that during some set of consecutive days, the champion must play exactly seven matches.

Project 12

In a certain society, each young woman is introduced to three young men on her eighteenth birthday. The three young men have been selected by her parents as worthy suitors. All the young men selected at all are selected by at least three families to meet their daughters.

Prove that it is always possible for every selected boy to marry a girl to whom he has been introduced.

Project 13

The Tower of Hanoi is a well-known game in which disks of different sizes are transferred from one of three spikes to another, without a larger disk ever being placed on top of a smaller disk. At the start of the game, the disks are stacked on one of the three spikes, with the largest disk on the bottom and the smaller disks arranged above in order of size. All three spikes are used as the disks are slowly transferred from one spike to another.

The number of moves taken to transfer a certain number of disks may depend to a certain extent on the ability of the player. However, there is a definite minimum to the number of moves required for any given number of disks.

Beginning with three disks, determine the minimum number of moves required. Then use four disks, five disks, etc. As you gather your data, look for a pattern.

Find a formula for the minimum number of moves required to transfer a pile of n disks to one of the two other possible locations.

Project 14

A marketing firm proposes the use of a contest to motivate customers to buy a certain product. Every time a customer buys the product, a numbered card is included in the packaging. By collecting a complete set of these n

cards, the customer can win a prize worth $100. The product is chewing gum, costing $0.35 per pack.

The marketing company must determine the number of customers likely to win a $100 prize during the run of the advertising campaign, which will market one million packs of gum.

Determine

(a) the number of packages of gum a customer must buy on the average in order to collect a full set of n different gum cards, if the cards are randomly packaged with the gum.

(b) the total amount that the gum costs the customer.

(c) the number of prizes likely to be claimed during the campaign.

4

FIBONACCI NUMBERS

Leonardo Fibonacci was born in 1175 and received a portion of his education at the hands of the Muslims of Barbary. From them he learned the Arabic (decimal) system of numeration and Alkarismi's system of algebra. Returning to his home country of Italy, he published a book in 1202, *Liber Abaci*, which for 200 years was the principal means of introducing the Hindu-Arabic system of numeration to Christian Europeans.

Today, Fibonacci is most frequently associated with a **sequence,** or list, of numbers found in *Liber Abaci*. This sequence is known as the **Fibonacci sequence.** Its terms begin as follows:

$$1, 1, 2, 3, 5, 8, 13, 21, 34, 55, \ldots \text{ etc.}$$

Notice that each term in the sequence equals the sum of the previous two terms. For example, 5 equals 2 plus 3; 8 equals 3 plus 5; 13 equals 5 plus 8; etc.

The sequence is presented in Fibonacci's book in connection with a discussion of the breeding of rabbits. Strangely, if one starts with a pair of breeding rabbits capable of producing a pair of offspring every month, and if these offspring and all their progeny breed within one month of their own births and every month thereafter, then month-by-month totals of each of the following categories all contain the Fibonacci sequence: pairs of breeding rabbits at the beginning of each month, pairs of nonbreeding rabbits at the beginning of each month, pairs of rabbits bred during each month, pairs of rabbits living at the end of each month.

Fibonacci numbers and other topics found in this chapter are particularly interesting to many people because of the curious ways in which they seem to characterize the properties of certain natural objects and processes in nature. For example, Fibonacci numbers also can be used to describe the genealogy of honeybees, the positioning of leaves around plant stems (phyllotaxis), the spiral patterns found in the heads of sunflowers, and many other natural phenomena.

Fibonacci numbers also emerge quite unexpectedly in a wide range of purely abstract mathematical activities. It is the recurrence of these mathematical curiosities in seemingly unrelated contexts that motivates many researchers to continue the search for new insights into the Fibonacci numbers.

LUCAS NUMBERS

The French mathematician Edouard Lucas lived during the latter half of the nineteenth century. In 1877, Lucas created the sequnce now named the **Lucas sequence:**

$$1, 3, 4, 7, 11, 18, 29, 47, 76, \ldots \text{ etc.}$$

Notice that this sequence also creates terms by finding the sum of the previous two terms. Compare Lucas's sequence with Fibonacci's sequence. Some rather interesting relationships can be quickly identified. Verify them

FIBONACCI NUMBERS CAN BE USED TO DESCRIBE
THE SPIRAL PATTERN OF THE SEEDS IN A SUNFLOWER
AND OF THE LEAVES OF THE CACTUS SHOWN HERE.

MORE SPIRALS IN NATURE: CHRISTMAS FERN
FIDDLEHEADS, A WHELK SHELL, AND A NEW ENGLAND
NEPTUNE SHELL (COUNTERCLOCKWISE).

for yourself: (1) The product of each Fibonacci number with its corresponding Lucas number is another Fibonacci number. (2). When alternate (every other) terms of the Fibonacci sequence are added, the sums are Lucas numbers.

The following project ideas vary in difficulty. Among them you may find the seed of a research idea. Before committing yourself to any topic, however, check with your math teacher to verify that your selection is appropriate to your background and ability.

Project 15

What kinds of numbers do you get when you perform arithmetic and/or algebraic operations on the Fibonacci numbers? Use addition, subtraction, multiplication, etc. Are Fibonacci numbers found among the results? What about the squares of Fibonacci numbers? cubes of Fibonacci numbers? etc.

Investigate the results obtained when Fibonacci numbers undergo transformation using common arithmetic and algebraic operations.

Project 16

You could ask the same question about Lucas numbers, so another problem can be stated similarly.

Investigate the results obtained when Lucas numbers undergo transformation using common arithmetic and algebraic operations.

Project 17

What about combinations of Lucas and Fibonacci numbers? You could try adding, subtracting, or multiplying corresponding Fibonacci and Lucas numbers.

Investigate the results obtained when Lucas and Fibonacci numbers are combined using common arithmetic and algebraic operations.

Project 18

A **series** is formed by taking the sum of the terms of a sequence. For instance, the Fibonacci numbers can be written as a series as follows:

$$1 + 1 + 2 + 3 + 5 + 8 + 13 + \ldots \text{ etc.}$$

A series such as this, having an infinite number of terms, is called an **infinite series.**

On the other hand, you can form a sum of only the first n Fibonacci numbers. A sequence of sums can then be formed by taking progressively longer and longer sums of the elements of the original Fibonacci sequence. By listing all such sums in order, a **sequence of partial sums** is created. For example,

Number of term (n):	1 2 3 4 5 6 . . . etc.
Fibonacci sequence:	1 1 2 3 5 8 . . . etc.
Sequence of partial sums:	1 2 4 7 12 20 . . . etc.
(sum of first n terms)	

Investigate the sequence of partial sums of the Fibonacci and Lucas sequences. Also consider various arithmetic and algebraic transformations of these sequences.

Project 19

Fibonacci numbers may be generated using Pascal's triangle. First consider the conventional manner for writing Pascal's triangle (Table 1).

Table 1
Pascal's Triangle

```
        1   1
      1   2   1
    1   3   3   1
  1   4   6   4   1
1   5  10  10   5   1
        etc.
```

Rewrite Table 1 in columns and rows as shown in Table 2.

Table 2
Pascal's Triangle
in Columns and Rows

```
1  1
1  2   1
1  3   3   1
1  4   6   4   1
1  5  10  10   5   1
        etc.
```

Now examine the sums of the numbers found along diagonals in Table 2. For instance, beginning at the lower-left corner of the table, $1 + 4 + 3 = 8$, a Fibonacci number. Also, beginning just above the same point, $1 + 3 + 1 = 5$, another Fibonacci number.

Investigate this phenomenon for an expanded Pascal's triangle.

Determine

(a) which diagonal sums will produce sums which are Fibonacci numbers.

(b) if sums taken along diagonals drawn in different directions also produce Fibonacci numbers.

(c) if Lucas numbers appear in the table or sums of its terms.

Project 20

Examine the Fibonacci and Lucas sequences with respect to **prime numbers** (a number evenly divisible only by itself and 1). Does each sequence contain primes? Do you think that an infinite number of primes exists in each sequence or do you think there is a last prime in each sequence?

Investigate whether the Fibonacci and Lucas sequences contain an infinite number of prime numbers or if there is a largest prime in each sequence.

Project 21
S.M. Ulam constructed a sequence of positive integers having the property that each number in the sequence can be expressed as the sum of exactly two earlier numbers in the sequence, that is, in only *one* way. The sequence begins as follows:

1, 2, 3, 4, 6, 8, 11, 13, 16, 18, 26, 28, . . . etc.

Examine the Fibonacci and Lucas numbers. Investigate whether all the numbers in each sequence can be expressed as the sum of at most two Ulam numbers.

Project 22
Determine which Fibonacci numbers, if any, are equal to half the difference or sum of two cubes.

Project 23
Pretend that you have a large suply of pennies. Place one on a flat surface. Below the first penny, place a row of two pennies, forming a triangle. Below this row, place a third row of three pennies, once again forming a triangle. Continue this process, each row having one more penny in it than the previous row.

Now consider the number of pennies in each triangle formed in this manner. The first penny, by itself, represents a figure with one penny in it. The addition of a second row forms a triangle with three pennies in it. The first three rows form a triangle consisting of six pennies. If this process is continued, each additional row generating a larger triangle, the number of pennies in each triangle forms a sequence of **triangular numbers.**

The sequence of triangular numbers begins as follows:

1, 3, 6, 10, 15, 21, 28 . . . etc.

It is known that every whole number is either a triangular number, the sum of two triangular numbers, or the sum of three triangular numbers. You can also think of this in another way: given any whole number, you can always form one, two, or three triangles using the given number of markers.

Determine whether any Fibonacci numbers are triangular. If so, investigate whether there are infinitely many triangular Fibonacci numbers or only a few. Answer the same questions with respect to the Lucas numbers.

Project 24

There are many examples of Fibonacci numbers in nature. What about Lucas numbers?

Explore nature and its processes with an eye for Fibonacci and Lucas numbers. Keep records—notes and sketches—of any patterns that you find.

Project 25

A common topic in second-year algebra is matrices and determinants.

Investigate the properties of matrices and determinants having consecutive Fibonacci or Lucas numbers as entries.

Project 26

If you perform the indicated division in the expression $x/(1-x-x^2)$, you obtain as a quotient the polynomial expression

$$1x + 1x^2 + 2x^3 + 5x^5 + 8x^6 + 13x^7 + \ldots$$

Notice that the coefficients are the elements of the Fibonacci sequence.

Look for other expressions which yield Fibonacci numbers in the form of coefficients to polynomial expressions.

Look for an expression which yields Lucas numbers in the same fashion.

Project 27

Binet developed an expression for the $(n+1)$th term of the Fibonacci sequence. It is

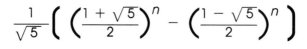

$$\frac{1}{\sqrt{5}}\left(\left(\frac{1 + \sqrt{5}}{2}\right)^n - \left(\frac{1 - \sqrt{5}}{2}\right)^n \right)$$

for $n = 0,1,2, \ldots$

A similar formula may or may not exist for the Lucas numbers. Investigate this possibility.

THE GOLDEN SECTION

Given any line segment, say, from point A to point B, there are infinitely many ways that you could cut or partition the segment into two sections. Among those many ways, however, there is one way thought to produce a division more beautiful than all the rest. To the Greeks, this special partition was called the golden section. Other names also exist: the golden ratio, the golden cut, and the divine proportion.

Stated in the form of a proportion, a segment AB is divided according to the golden section at point C when $AB/AC = AC/CB$.

    A_____C_____B

You can approximate the ratio AC/CB by forming the ratio of any two successive Fibonacci numbers, the larger of the two numbers being the numerator of the ratio (see Project 29). By selecting larger and larger Fibonacci number pairs, the resulting approximation of the golden ratio becomes more and more accurate.

THE PARTHENON, PICTURED HERE, IS ONE OF
THE MOST FAMOUS OF ANCIENT GREEK BUILDINGS.

Many people feel that rectangles constructed with this proportion in mind (length $= AC$, width $= CB$) are more appealing than rectangles with other proportions. Rectangles with "golden proportions" are called golden rectangles. An isosceles triangle with sides of length AB and base of length CB is called a golden triangle.

Project 28
Test the popularity of golden rectangles and golden triangles relative to other rectangles and triangles experimentally. Ask experimental subjects to select a favorite rectangle and triangle from a set of drawings containing a wide variety of rectangles and triangles. Compare the frequency with which the "golden" shapes are selected to the frequency of selection for the other shapes. Perform a statistical analysis of the results.

Project 29

When the golden ratio, *AC/CB*, is calculated, the value 1.618033988 . . . is obtained. This number is commonly represented by the Greek letter ϕ, or **phi** (say "fee"). This number has fascinated mathematicians for centuries. For example, consider the powers of ϕ found in Table 3.

Table 3
Powers of ϕ

$$\phi^1 = 1\phi + 0$$
$$\phi^2 = 1\phi + 1$$
$$\phi^3 = 2\phi + 1$$
$$\phi^4 = 3\phi + 2$$
$$\phi^5 = 5\phi + 3$$
$$\phi^6 = 8\phi + 5$$

Examine the column of coefficients of ϕ. Examine the column of constants. Both columns contain the Fibonacci sequence!

Now take any two consecutive Fibonacci numbers, say 55 and 34. Divide the larger number by the smaller. In this case, $55/34 = 1.617647059$. Try several other divisions using larger and larger Fibonacci numbers. What happens?

Investigate the relationships between the Fibonacci numbers and phi. Use the insights you gain to predict the value of the ninety-ninth power of ϕ.

Project 30

Investigate the relationships among the Fibonacci numbers, golden rectangles, and logarithmic spirals.

Project 31

Investigate whether the sides of a polygon can ever be consecutive Fibonacci or Lucas numbers.

5

NUMBER THEORY

Number theory has been a recreational pursuit for mathematicians for centuries. Because it is so easy to "get into" yet so immensely deep, the possibilities for research in this area are outstanding even for beginners. The topics discussed in this chapter do not begin to outline the full possibilities of this discipline, so be sure to do some investigation on your own.

SYSTEMS OF NUMERATION

Many interesting questions can be asked about numbers in bases other than base 10. When investigating such questions, it is often necessary to convert numbers from one base to another. Converting numbers from one **system of numeration** (base) to another can be time-consuming. To make this aspect of your research easier, here's a computer program written in BASIC which converts numbers from some other base to base 10.

```
5 REM CONVERT TO BASE 10
10 REM THIS PROGRAM CONVERTS FROM ANY BASE TO
     BASE 10
```

```
20 REM FIRST ENTER THE BASE YOU WISH TO CHANGE
     FROM.
30 REM THEN ENTER THE NUMBER AS IT IS WRITTEN IN THAT
     BASE
40 INPUT "BASE TO CHANGE FROM "; BF
50 INPUT "HOW MANY DIGITS IN YOUR NUMBER" ; ND
60 DIM D(ND), VL(ND) : REM ENTER THE DIGITS LEFT TO
     RIGHT
70 FOR I = ND TO 1 STEP −1
80 INPUT "ENTER DIGIT "; D(I)
90 NEXT I
100 REM COMPUTE THE VALUE OF EACH COLUMN, LEFT
     TO RIGHT
110 REM AND KEEP A RUNNING TOTAL OF THE COLUMNS
120 FOR I = ND TO 1 STEP −1
130 VL(I) = D(I) * BF^(I − 1)
140 TTL = TTL + VL(I)
150 NEXT I
160 REM PRINT THE ANSWER
170 PRINT "THE NUMBER IN BASE 10 NOTATION IS "; TTL
```

Project 32

In addition to this program, you might want a BASIC program which converts numbers from base 10 to any other base. In order to give you a clue how this can be done, the following BASIC program shows how to convert from base 10 to base 2. When you modify this program to convert from base 10 to some other base, you will need to add a few lines and modify the lines containing the notation :REM ?

```
10 REM CONVERTS FROM BASE 10 TO BASE 2      :REM ?
20 REM ENTER THE BASE 10 NUMBER
30 INPUT "ENTER THE BASE 10 NUMBER "; N
40 REM FIND THE LARGEST BASE 2 DIVISOR      :REM ?
50 D = 1
60 AD = 1
70 Q = N/D
```

```
80 IF INT(Q) = 1 THEN GOTO 120
90 D = 2 * D                                    :REM ?
100 AD = AD + 1
110 GOTO 70
120 REM LARGEST BASE 2 DIVISOR = CURRENT DIVISOR
                                                :REM ?
130 REM BEGIN CONVERTING TO BASE 2              :REM ?
140 FOR I = AD TO 1 STEP −1
150 IF N/D >= 1 THEN PRINT "1"; : N = N − D : GOTO 170
                                                :REM ?
160 IF N/D < 1 THEN PRINT "0";
170 ND = D/2                                    :REM ?
180 D = ND
190 NEXT I
```

Once you can convert numbers from one base to another, you will need some questions to explore. Here are a few for starters.

Project 33

When the same sequence of digits, say, 1011101, is used to represent numbers in several bases, how do the base 10 equivalents of those numbers compare? Are there any numbers that look the same in every number base? In at least two number bases? At least three? For example, how do the base 10 equivalents of the following numbers compare: 3_{three}, 3_{four}, 3_{five}?

Investigate the written forms of a wide range of numbers in several systems of numeration. Look for numbers which are identical in more than one system of numeration.

Project 34

In base 10, a simple test can be applied to any integer to determine if it is divisible by 3. To use the test, simply add the digits in the integer to obtain a new integer. Repeat this until a single digit is obtained. If this digit is divisible by 3, then the original number is divisible by 3. For example, is 1,234 divisible by 3?

Following the rules of this test, $1 + 2 + 3 + 4 = 10$. This is a two-digit number. Both digits are added to obtain the sum $1 + 0 = 1$. Since 1 is not divisible by 3, the test informs us that 1,234 is not divisible by 3.

Investigate the divisibility-by-3 check in other systems of numeration. Determine

(a) if this rule works in any other systems of numeration.
(b) what correcting modifications are possible if it does not work "as is."
(c) if similar divisibility checks for other divisors are possible.

CODE CONSCIOUS

Once you have solved the problem of converting from base 10 to any other base, you can try your luck at a little secret-code work. One of the simplest ways to code a message has been to assign each letter of the alphabet a number. For instance, you might simply use the code key found in Table 4.

Table 4
Secret Code Key

Symbol	Code	Symbol	Code	Symbol	Code
A	1	K	11	U	21
B	2	L	12	V	22
C	3	M	13	W	23
D	4	N	14	X	24
E	5	O	15	Y	25
F	6	P	16	Z	26
G	7	Q	17	?	27
H	8	R	18	,	28
I	9	S	19	.	29
J	10	T	20	space	30

Simply substitute the code number for each letter. For instance, the message "MEET ME AFTER SCHOOL" would be coded as follows:

MEET = 13 5 5 20   ME = 13 4   AFTER = 1 6 20 5 18
SCHOOL = 19 3 8 15 15 12

Using the code for a space, the message becomes

13 5 5 20 30 13 4 30 1 6 20 5 18 30 19 3 8 15 15 12

Project 35
Write a computer CODE program in BASIC to do the message coding and decoding for you!

Project 36
On the other hand, it wouldn't take a teacher long to "crack" the code, especially a teacher with a computer. It's too simple.
    Make the code more complicated by changing the code numbers. You could start with A = 3, then B = 4, C = 5, etc. Modify your computer CODE program to allow for different starting numbers for A.

Project 37
Can you make your CODE program crack any code based on such a scheme? Wouldn't the letter A always be the smallest number in the code key? Wouldn't the letter B always be the next to smallest number in the key? Just how long would such a code be secret?
    A more complex code key might scramble the numbers and letters they represent randomly. Such a code would be much more difficult to crack. Modify your BASIC code program to scramble the symbols randomly.

Project 38
An even more secret code could begin with the key found in Table 4. Once the message is coded, the num-

bers could be converted to a different number base using the suggested modification to the CONVERTS FROM BASE 10 TO BASE 2 program previously discussed. The base in which the code is written could be embedded in the message itself as, say, the first or second or last number. The receiver of the message would then merely use the CONVERTS TO BASE 10 program to decode the message prior to using Table 4. Such a code is much more difficult to crack as its number base can change with every message.

Modify your code program to make use of this strategy.

PRIME TIME

As you may know, a prime number is a whole number which is evenly divisible only by itself and 1. The list of primes begins 2, 3, 5, 7, 11, 13, . . . etc. If you want to determine whether a given number is prime, such as 47, you can always find out by dividing it by every number less than itself, beginning with 2. One the other hand, this is an unnecessary "overkill."

Project 39

Investigate the process of testing a number to determine if it is prime. Develop a procedure which does not waste time and effort by doing unnecessary calculations.

Project 40

Write a computer program that lists the primes. Print a list of a hundred primes. (You may need a lot of computer time to do this!). Examine the digits in the rightmost and leftmost positions in prime numbers to determine if (a) certain digits are more likely to occur in the rightmost or leftmost positions in primes, (b) if they occur in non-primes, (c) if nonprimes have other features which can make their identification easier.

37	36	35	34	33	32	31
38	17	16	15	14	13	30
39	18	5	4	3	12	29
40	19	6	1	2	11	28
41	20	7	8	9	10	27
42	21	22	23	24	25	26
43						

Figure 1. Prime number grid

Project 41

Convert a large list of primes to several other number bases. Investigate whether the primes are any easier to identify in the other systems of numeration.

Project 42

Using an extended version of the grid in Figure 1 as a reference, mark the primes, noting where they tend to fall. Look for patterns of primes falling on (a) rows, (b) columns, (c) diagonals. Create a variety of reference grids and repeat the investigations.

Project 43

Another approach to prime-testing makes use of Wilson's theorem: N is prime if $(N-1)! + 1$ is divisible by N. The symbol ! is read "factorial." To illustrate its meaning, $3! =$

$1 \times 2 \times 3 = 6$ and $6! = 1 \times 2 \times 3 \times 4 \times 5 \times 6 = 720$. As you can see, the factorial function can generate some mighty big numbers.

Now let's try Wilson's theorem out on the number 5. According to this theorem, 5 is prime if $(5-1)! + 1$ is divisible by 5. Since $(5-1)! + 1 = 4! + 1 = 24 + 1 = 25$, and since 25 is divisible by 5, Wilson's theorem seems to work for the number 5. What about for the number 29? Here, indeed, is a job for a calculator or computer.

Write a BASIC program to do the calculations for Wilson's theorem. Just a warning: most microcomputers will run out of memory quickly on such calculations.

Project 44

Wilson's theorem can be used easily on calculators having the factorial function. The factorial calculator key normally has the symbol $n!$ printed on it.

Use Wilson's theorem and a calculator to test the following assertion: If n is prime, then $n! + 1$ is prime. Investigate the possibility that there is a largest prime.

Project 45

A **superprime** is a prime number having an additional interesting feature: every integer obtained by deleting an arbitrary number of rightmost digits is itself prime. For example, the number 7331 is a superprime. Delete the 1 and the new integer is 733, a prime. Delete the 31 and the new integer is 73, a prime. Delete the 331 and the new integer is 7, a prime. The integers 317 and 2399 are also superprimes.

Investigate superprimes. Make a list. If you can program in BASIC, write a program to find superprimes. Examine superprimes for (a) any digits which never appear, (b) any digits which always appear in a superprime. Investigate whether there is (a) an infinite number of superprimes, (b) a largest superprime, (c) a rule like Wilson's theorem for superprimes.

Project 46
The Goldbach **conjecture** (in mathematics, a conjecture is a powerful hunch) states that every even integer n greater than or equal to 6 is the sum of two odd primes and every odd integer n greater than or equal to 9 is the sum of three odd primes.

Test the Goldbach conjecture by writing a computer program which will do the necessary trial-and-error calculations.

Project 47
Investigate the proportion of primes occurring in an interval from 2 to n. As n gets larger, what happens to the proportion, or percentage, of integers in the interval which are prime. Find a mathematical expression which approximates or predicts this proportion.

Project 48
Investigate primes formed by squaring an integer and adding 1, $n^2 + 1$, and whether there are infinitely many such primes.

Project 49
The following expressions generate primes:

$$3! - 2! + 1! = 5$$
$$4! - 3! + 2! - 1! = 19$$
$$5! - 4! + 3! - 2! + 1! = 101$$

Investigate whether all such expressions generate primes.

PERFECT NUMBERS

A **perfect number** is defined as one that equals the sum of all its divisors (other than itself). For example, 6 is divisible by 1, 2, and 3, and $1 + 2 + 3 = 6$. The next perfect number is 28. Altogether, only thirty perfect numbers are known, the largest having 130,100 digits!

Since the times of Euclid, it has been known that the expression $2^{n-1}(2^n-1)$ generates even perfect numbers whenever 2^n-1 is a prime. Numbers generated by the expression 2^n-1 are called Mersenne numbers. So, finding even perfect numbers with this expression involves a study of Mersenne primes as well as "perfection." In fact, every time a new Mersenne prime is discovered, a new perfect number is automatically found.

The study of perfect numbers has already won Michael Friedman third prize in the 1985 Westinghouse Science Talent Search. Here indeed is a topic worth investigating.

Project 50
Euclid's formula always produces even perfect numbers. The mathematician Leonhard Euler proved that it would produce every even perfect number. Michael Friedman proved that there are no odd perfect numbers less than 10^{79}.

Investigate whether there may be any odd perfect numbers.

Project 51
There is an "odd" connection between perfect numbers (other than the first, 6) and the sum of cubes of consecutive odd numbers. Consider the following examples:

$$28 = 1^3 + 3^3$$
$$496 = 1^3 + 3^3 + 5^3 + 7^3$$
$$8128 = 1^3 + 3^3 + 5^3 + 7^3 + 9^3 + 11^3 + 13^3 + 15^3$$

Investigate this pattern and whether it is true for all perfect numbers.

6

SEQUENCES
AND SERIES

There are a number of interesting contexts in which you can study sequences and series of integers, fractions, and decimals. Little mathematical sophistication is required beyond algebra and the method of proof known as mathematical induction.

For most of the problems in this chapter, an inductive approach works quite well: gather data and list it in columns in a table; look for a relationship between the columns; once a relationship is determined and tested on a few data points, try to prove it using mathematical induction.

The following example illustrates a problem which can be studied using these concepts and skills.

SUMMING A FINITE
NUMBER OF TERMS

A staircase pattern is to be created using blocks arranged as shown in Figure 2.

The problem is to find a formula which will calculate the total number of blocks in the staircase from the number of steps in the staircase. The formula should convert

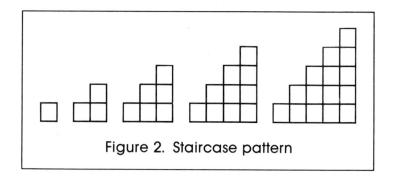

Figure 2. Staircase pattern

any number in the first column into its corresponding number in the last column. See Table 5 for examples.

You can quickly see from Figure 2 and Table 5 that adding another step (dropping down one row in the table) adds the same number of blocks to the staircase as the number of blocks under the new step (the number in the middle column of the new row). For instance, adding the fifth step added five blocks to the total number of blocks required for four steps.

At this point, you should realize that the nth number in the column on the right equals the sum of the first n numbers in the middle column. This can be represented by the series 1 + 2 + 3 + 4 + 5 + . . . etc.

Table 5

No. of Steps	No. Under Top Step	Total No. of Blocks
1	1	1
2	2	3
3	3	6
4	4	10
5	5	15
6	?	?
7	?	?
	etc.	

This observation is not a satisfactory solution to the problem. What if somebody asks how many blocks would be necessary to build a staircase having sixty-eight steps? You don't want to extend the series that far, do you? You'd have to add all the integers from 1 to 68. What you need is a formula of some kind which takes the number 68 and produces the number of blocks in the staircase.

Project 52

One formula for the sum of n terms (a staircase with n steps) in the series $1 + 2 + 3 + \ldots + n$ is

$$1 + 2 + 3 + \ldots + n = (n^2 + n)/2.$$

Demonstrate that this formula works for several different values of n. For example, show that the number of boxes needed for a sixty-eight-step staircase is equal to $1 + 2 + 3 + \ldots + 68 = (68^2 + 68)/2$. Derive the formula using the technique of finite differences, then prove it using mathematical induction.

Project 53

Figure 3 shows a series of box diagrams. How many boxes can you see in each diagram? The second diagram contains five boxes, the four small boxes plus the one large

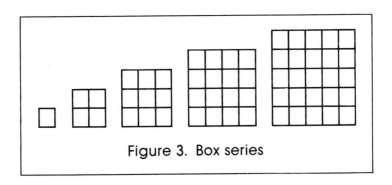

Figure 3. Box series

box defined by the outside shape of the diagram. How many boxes do you see in the diagram with three small boxes on a side? With four small boxes on a side? Etc.

Generate a data table for this problem. Represent the number of boxes visible in a square array of boxes as a series. Then find a formula which will calculate the number of boxes to be found in every such array of boxes. Prove the formula using mathematical induction.

Project 54

Figure 4 uses triangles in a similar context. How many triangles can you see in each diagram?

Follow the same procedures indicated in the previous problem. Your purpose is to find a formula which will calculate the number of triangles to be found in an *n*-tiered array of equilateral triangles. Prove the formula using mathematical induction.

Project 55

Design several geometric figures such as those shown in Figures 2, 3, and 4; then find a formula for each which serves the same purpose as those in the three previous projects. Prove your results.

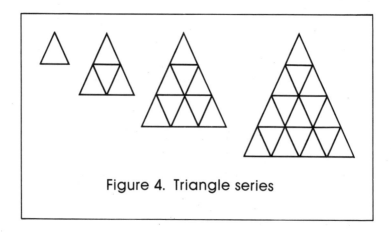

Figure 4. Triangle series

Project 56

Imagine a plane, flat and infinite. Draw one line, straight and infinite, in the plane. Your line divides the plane into two plane parts. Now add a second line. Depending on where you add the second line, the plane is divided into either three or four separate plane parts.

What happens when you add a third line? Does the number of plane parts obtained depend upon where you place your third line? What rule will you use for positioning additional lines so that the maximum number of plane parts is obtained each time?

Keep adding lines and counting plane parts until you have solved the following problem:

Find a formula for calculating the maximum number of parts into which two-dimensional space (a plane) can be divided using n straight lines. Prove your result using mathematical induction.

Project 57

Imagine a plane, flat and infinite. Draw a circle in the plane. The circle divides the plane into two plane parts. Now add a second circle in such a manner as to produce the maximum number of plane parts. Continue adding circles, each time making sure the placement of the next circle results in the maximum number of plane parts.

Keep adding circles and counting plane parts until you have enough data to justify a generalization.

Find a formula for calculating the maximum number of parts into which a plane can be divided using n circles. Prove your result using mathematical induction.

Project 58

This problem concerns the partition of infinite, three-dimensional space into regions. Begin by imagining empty space, extending infinitely far in every direction. Draw in a flat, infinite plane. The plane divides space into two regions. Now add a second plane. Add a third and a fourth, each time making sure that the maximum number of regions is obtained. Continue adding planes in this manner until you can justify a generalization.

Find a formula for calculating the maximum number of regions into which three-dimensional space can be divided using n planes.

Project 59
Repeat the process in the problem above, this time using spheres to partition three-dimensional space. Continue adding spheres in this manner until you can answer the following problem: Find a formula for calculating the maximum number of regions into which three-dimensional space can be divided using n spheres.

JUST NUMBERS
You can study finite sequences and series without reference to geometric considerations. The following projects are examples of studies of finite number sums and sequences. Where appropriate, generate a table of data, represent the desired answer as a series, and find a formula for the sum of the series.

Project 60
Find an expression for the sum of the square of n integers. For example, if n equals 4, find the sum $1^2 + 2^2 + 3^2 + 4^2$ using a formula. Prove your result using mathematical induction.

Project 61
Investigate the sum of the cubes of n integers. Find an expression which calculates the sum; then prove it using mathematical induction.

Project 62
Investigate the series $2^1 + 2^2 + 2^3 + \ldots + 2^n$. Find an expression to calculate the sum of n terms of this series. Prove your results using mathematical induction.

Project 63

Investigate similar series using bases other than 2. In each case find a formula to calculate the sum of *n* terms of the series.

Project 64

In an **arithmetic sequence**, there is a constant difference between successive terms. For instance, the sequence 2, 5, 8, 11, 14 is constructed with a common difference of three between terms.

Investigate whether an arithmetic sequence of primes could be of any length.

Project 65

Investigate whether an arithmetic sequence of consecutive primes could be of any length.

Project 66

One of the oldest written mathematical documents from antiquity is the Rhind papyrus from Egypt. It deals with the representation of fractions as the sum of a series of unit fractions. For example,

$$\frac{2}{7} = \frac{1}{5} + \frac{1}{13} + \frac{1}{115} + \frac{1}{10465}$$

Investigate this, varying the number of unitary fractions in the sum. Look for generalizations.

WHEN YOU HAVE AN INFINITE NUMBER OF TERMS

The series $1/2 + 1/4 + 1/8 + \ldots$ is called an infinite series because it has infinitely many terms. This series is said to **converge** to the value 1. This means that as you add more and more terms, the sum gets closer and closer to 1. No finite number of these terms would ever equal or exceed 1, but you can get as close as you want. This is sometimes written as $1/2 + 1/4 + 1/8 + \ldots = 1$.

Other infinite series do not converge to a number. As you add more terms, the sum becomes larger and larger without bound. For example, $1/2 + 1/3 + 1/4 + \ldots = \infty$.

Mathematicians frequently are interested in whether a particular series converges. Answering such questions can take real insight and creativity.

Project 67
Investigate the infinite series $1 + 1/2 + 1/3 + 1/4 + 1/5 + 1/6 + \ldots + 1/n + \ldots$. Prove that this series does not converge.

Project 68
Show that

$$\frac{1}{3} = \frac{1}{2^2} + \frac{1}{2^4} + \frac{1}{2^6} + \frac{1}{2^8} + \ldots$$

Look for other expressions of a similar nature.

Project 69
Investigate various mathematical models for vibrating or bouncing objects. Describe the total distances bounced or vibrated using infinite series.

Project 70
A simple continued fraction has the form

$$a_1 + \cfrac{1}{a_2 + \cfrac{1}{a_3 + \cfrac{1}{a_4 + \ldots \text{ etc.}}}}$$

For example, it is known that

$$\sqrt{2} = 1 + \cfrac{1}{2 + \cfrac{1}{2 + \cfrac{1}{2 + \cfrac{1}{2 + \ldots \text{ etc.}}}}}$$

Demonstrate that the above continued fraction does converge to 2. Look for other convergent continued fractions.

Project 71
Prove true or false: If p_n is the nth prime, then $\Sigma(-1)n_n/p_n$ converges.

7

GEOMETRY AND TOPOLOGY

Early in the eighteenth century in East Prussia, the people of the city of Koenigsberg strolled along the River Pregel and puzzled whether it was possible, crossing each bridge once and only once, to walk a complete circuit of the seven bridges connecting the two islands in the river with each other and the riverbanks. Figure 5 illustrates the relationship of the bridges to the river and its banks.

In 1736, the great mathematician Leonhard Euler solved the Koenigsberg bridge problem in a paper which marks the beginning of a branch of mathematics known as graph theory. Euler realized that the problem could be illustrated more conveniently using a drawing that reduced the land to points and the bridges to lines (Figure 6). Such a diagram is called a **network**.

A network is said to be **traversable** if it is possible to start at some point and traverse (follow along) every line once and only once until all the lines have been traversed. Using this concept, the Koenigsberg bridge problem can be restated: is the Koenigsberg bridge network traversable?

Euler concluded that the Koenigsberg network is not traversable by proving that all networks having more

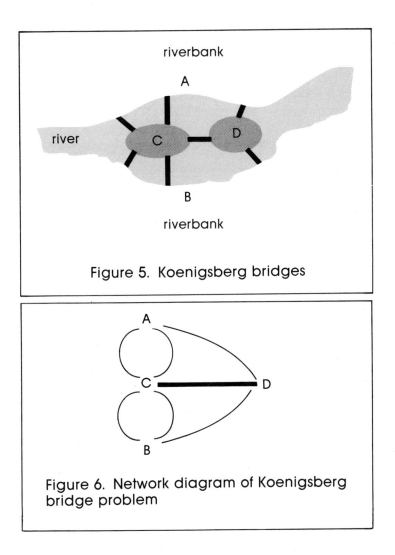

Figure 5. Koenigsberg bridges

Figure 6. Network diagram of Koenigsberg bridge problem

than two odd vertices are not traversable. An odd vertex is a point on a network at which an odd number of lines come together. An even vertex is a point at which an even number of lines come together. When traversing a network with two odd vertices, you must start at one odd

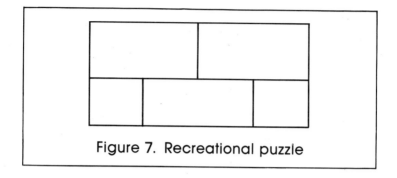

Figure 7. Recreational puzzle

vertex and end at the other. When traversing a network with all even vertices, you may start at any vertex, ending at the same point. As you can see by examining Figure 6, all four of the Koenigsberg network vertices are odd.

Figure 7 may look familiar. As a mathematical recreation, it has often been asked if it is possible to draw a pencil line through each of the line segments in the diagram once and only once without lifting the pencil from the paper. You can use the same approach as Euler in addressing this brainteaser.

Project 72

Redraw the puzzle as a network, as Euler did, then decide if the network is traversable. Continue to investigate this method of analysis by constructing and analyzing a wide variety of similar puzzles and their network diagrams.

Project 73

A related problem is that of the traveling salesperson. Figure 8 shows a map of the sales territory of a certain traveling salesperson. The salesperson's problem is not to traverse every road (line), but to reach every town (point), ideally with a minimum amount of driving.

A **Hamilton line** is a circuit or loop that passes

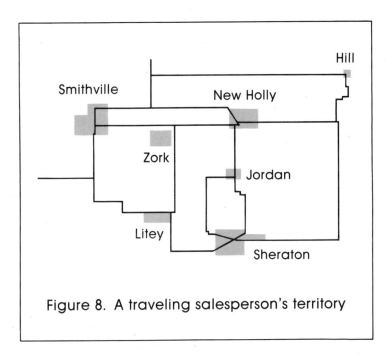

Figure 8. A traveling salesperson's territory

through each vertex of a graph exactly once. In general, such a line does not traverse all the lines of a graph.

Using Euler's discovery, you can determine if a graph is traversable by checking the vertices. Unfortunately, no comparable rule has been discovered for Hamilton lines.

Investigate the problem of the traveling salesman in the context of a study of Hamilton lines. Use a map of your county or state. Look for Hamilton lines between the major cities and towns.

Project 74

Here's another problem for the chess players. Determine if it is possible to move a knight around the entire chess board so that it occupies each square once and only once and returns at last to its starting position. Investigate this using the concept of a Hamilton line.

EXPERIMENTING WITH CONVENTIONAL KNOTS
MAY LEAD YOU TO SOME INTERESTING
DISCOVERIES ABOUT PAPER KNOTS.

KNOTTY PROBLEMS

Knot tying is a time-honored art for seamen, Boy Scouts, mothers, and a lot of other people trying to keep things together. But knots can generate some interesting and unexpected geometrical forms as well when they are tied using strips of paper rather than string or rope. Consider Figure 9.

In Figure 9, two strips of paper are folded over and interlaced at right angles. The result is a square. Another easy form to generate is the regular pentagon.

In Figure 10, a simple overhand knot in a single strip of paper produces a regular pentagon.

Project 75

Find paper knots that produce regular heptagons and octagons. Investigate whether other regular polygons can be generated using paper strips folded in this manner.

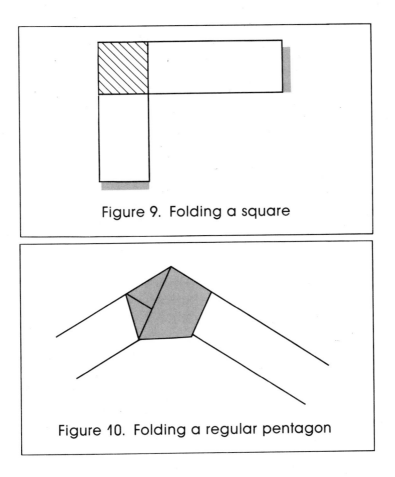

Figure 9. Folding a square

Figure 10. Folding a regular pentagon

Project 76

Gather three or more friends together. Face each other in a circle. Have everyone reach across the circle to join hands with one or two others, intertwining arms.

Investigate whether it is possible, without breaking grips, for the group to rearrange itself into a circle, each person holding hands with the people on his/her right and left. If this is possible, determine if it can always be done or if certain conditions must prevail.

"SWANS," A PAINTING BY M.C. ESCHER.
IS THIS A MOEBIUS STRIP?

TESSELLATIONS AND TILING

Have you seen any of M.C. Escher's drawings of interlocking soldiers, birds, fish, and other living creatures? The images fit together perfectly, leaving no space between them. Figures that "lock" together this way in the plane are called **tessellations**.

Many geometrical figures tessellate quite easily. Figure 11 shows two simple tessellations using regular polygons. Not all regular figures tessellate, however. There is no way to fit regular octagons together, for instance. However, a semiregular tessellation can be constructed using a combination of regular octagons and squares (See Figure 12).

Interesting tessellations can be created using combinations of straight and curved lines (see Figure 13). These tessellations make use of different symmetries to create interlocking figures.

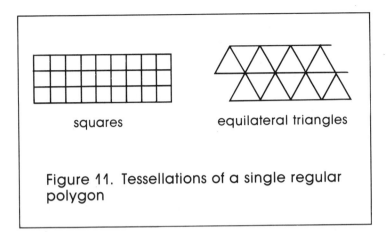

squares   equilateral triangles

Figure 11. Tessellations of a single regular polygon

THE COMPOUND EYE OF A FLY

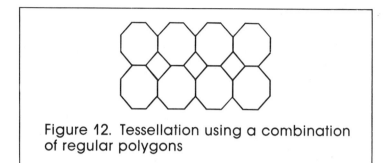

Figure 12. Tessellation using a combination of regular polygons

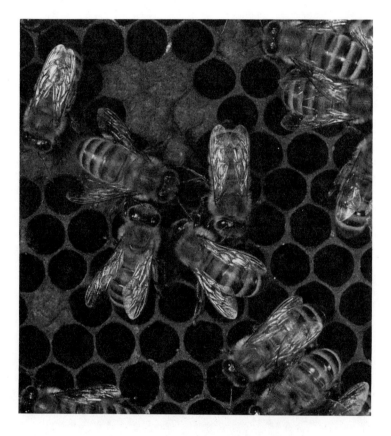

HONEYCOMB, WHOSE PATTERN IS FORMED
FROM TESSELLATING HEXAGONS

Figure 13. More-complex tessellations

SUNFLOWER SEEDS IN A TESSELLATING PATTERN
OF DIAMOND SHAPES; INTERLOCKING SHAPES
IN A SECTION OF A YUGOSLAVIAN RUG

PATTERNS IN TILES

Project 77

Investigate the symmetries that give rise to tessellating figures. Begin with simple figures and progress to more complex forms. Develop a series of generalizations concerning figures that tessellate. Relate your findings to the types of geometric variations you find in wallpaper patterns.

CURIOUS CURVES

In some manufacturing and transportation activities, materials are moved from one point to another along a track made of rollers. As the rollers turn, the materials are pushed along. Figure 14 illustrates such a situation.

In most cases, the rollers are cylindrical, having a round cross section. Strange as it may seem, there are other possible shapes for the rollers which would also convey the material along the track without causing it to wobble or bob up and down. All such cross-sectional shapes do have one feature in common, however. They are all curves of constant breadth.

Figure 15 illustrates the concept of the breadth of a closed curve. If a tangent is drawn to a curve at some point, *A*, and a perpendicular line drawn from point *A* into the interior of the curve, the perpendicular will intersect the curve at some other point, *B*. The distance

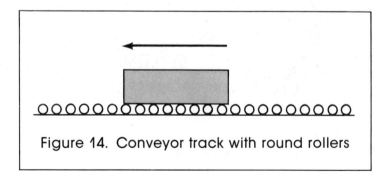

Figure 14. Conveyor track with round rollers

between point *A* and point *B* is the breadth of the curve in the direction of the perpendicular line.

If you try this with a circle, all the perpendicular lines pass through the center of the circle. This makes the lines all diameters.

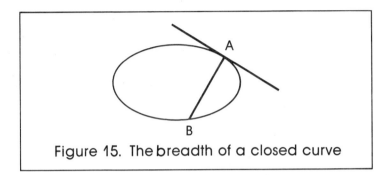

Figure 15. The breadth of a closed curve

ASSEMBLY LINE SHOWING ROLLERS

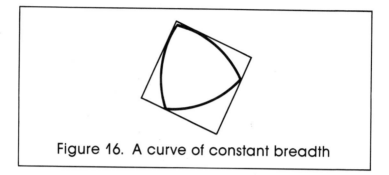

Figure 16. A curve of constant breadth

There are other curves, however, which also have the same breadth, no matter where the measurement is taken. Figure 16 illustrates such a curve.

The curve in Figure 16 is shown inside a square. Although it may be hard to accept on the basis of a diagram, the curve could rotate inside the square without any space to spare; that is, there would be no wobble.

Project 78
Curves of constant width having either an even or odd number of circular arcs are easy to draw using a compass. Investigate the relationship between the width and perimeters of curves having various numbers of "sides," or arcs. Investigate whether curves of constant width can be rotated inside shapes other than squares without wobble. Look for applications in science and engineering.

8

MISCELLANEOUS PROJECTS

This chapter presents a variety of unrelated project ideas. As in previous chapters, these projects vary in difficulty. Be sure to consult your mathematics teacher before making a final selection of a research topic.

PALINDROMES

Palindromes have the unusual quality of reading the same both forward and backward. For example,

ABLE WAS I ERE I SAW ELBA

or

56765

You can create numerical palindromes using the following set of rules:

1. Pick an integer, say, 97.
2. Reverse the digits and add to the original number: 97 + 79 = 176
3. Repeat the process: 176 + 671 = 847

4. Keep repeating the process:
$$847 + 748 = 1595$$
$$1595 + 5951 = 7546$$
$$7546 + 6457 = 14003$$
5. Eventually you will find a palindrome:
$$14003 + 30041 = 44044$$

Project 79

Prove that this process will always produce a palindrome. Search for a relationship between the original number and the number of steps needed to produce a palindrome.

Project 80

Table 6 shows an interesting sequence of palindromes created by squaring certain integers.

Table 6

$$1 \times 1 = 1$$
$$11 \times 11 = 121$$
$$111 \times 111 = 12321$$
$$1111 \times 1111 = 1234321$$
$$\text{etc.}$$

Investigate this sequence of squares. Determine if this procedure will always produce palindromes. Search for other procedures to generate palindromes by arithmetic and/or algebraic operations.

SLIPPERY SURFACES

NASA subcontracts with thousands of civilian companies to do research on specific problems related to the space program. Among the many subcontractors there is one individual who blows soap bubbles for NASA.

Soap films have the property of always assuming the form with the least possible surface area for the volume enclosed or the opening spanned. NASA thought this feature might be useful when designing the walls of space stations. So, NASA hired a bubble researcher.

Project 81
Investigate the surfaces created when wire forms of different shape are dipped in a soap, water, and glycerin solution. Find a way to record your observations. Look for applications in architecture, engineering, and space science.

MODEL BUILDING

Simply building a model of a polyhedron may not impress your teacher or the science fair judges, regardless of the amount of time you put in on the project. On the other hand, if you show originality in the selection and use of materials, everyone may pay attention.

Project 82
Investigate new methods and materials of creating three-dimensional models. Consider examples from nature of complex yet lightweight construction.

COMPUTER-BASED STUDIES

When selecting a research topic involving computers, be sure that you know how the topic has been handled by other researchers. The judges will not be impressed if you merely learn a variety of well-known computer tricks. Try to use the computer in a clever manner, not just as a brute force calculator. In other words, you should demonstrate originality in the way that you apply the technology. There are several ways to do that:

1. Use the computer to address a problem that has always been addressed in some other way. Your

use of the computer in the context of your research topic should be somewhat startling, demonstrating insight into previously unseen applications of this technology.

2. In the case of a research topic which has been addressed before using computers, find a new method of approaching the problem, using the computer in a new manner or as part of a new mathematical strategy.

3. Improve on some existing strategy by making the method of solution easier, faster, more accurate, etc.

One of the most interesting applications of computers is that of simulation and modeling. A computer model may be developed for almost any process for which there is a body of data. The purpose of the model is to imitate the actual process, predicting results in the real world. This is achieved by programming the computer to respond to various changes in data the same way that the actual, real-world process responds to changing conditions.

Project 83
Create a computer model to predict what will happen to cafeteria lunch lines in response to a variety of factors: food offered, day of the week, cost of items, etc.

Project 84
Create a computer model to predict changes in the buying habits of customers in a local shopping mall. Consider the effects of advertising, holidays, weather, etc. Work with the mall directors to obtain data.

Project 85
Build a computer model for a game of chance. Use the model to study winning strategies for the game.

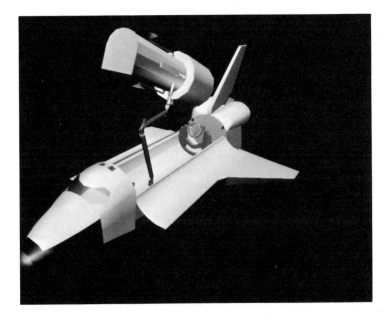

A COMPUTER-SIMULATED SPACESHIP

Project 86

Numerical analysis is a branch of mathematics dedicated to the discovery of new problem-solving techniques, particularly those involving a great deal of calculation. Select a topic in this area, say the calculation of volumes of irregularly shaped objects, and investigate new methods of obtaining solutions.

9

DYNAMICAL SYSTEMS, JULIA SETS, AND FRACTALS

Believe it or not, you may soon be begging your high school mathematics teacher for an introduction to dynamical systems and complex numbers. Among the other students sharing this interest, you may find future scientists, engineers, mathematicians, computer scientists, graphics designers, and artists. Artists?

LOOKING FOR BEAUTY
IN MATHEMATICS

If you have taken a second-year course in algebra, a course in trigonometry, or a course in analytic geometry, you probably have studied graphing. To many people, the circles, ellipses, parabolas, hyperbolas, and wave functions plotted in these courses have a kind of beauty arising from their clean, precise lines. On the other hand, you may have explored mathematically generated graphics using LOGO, creating complicated snowflake-like forms. Graphics generated in this manner often resemble forms and patterns found in nature and appeal to one's sense of design. Both of these attributes, clean lines and interesting patterns, illustrate the potential for beauty in mathematics.

LOGO SNOWFLAKES

A LOGO SNOWFLAKE
AND A REAL SNOWFLAKE

IT IS DIFFICULT TO MATCH THE
COMPLEXITY OF NATURE. THE
LOGO PROGRAMMER STILL HAS
A LOT OF WORK TO DO ON HER
DESIGN TO EVEN COME CLOSE.

The discovery that the study of mathematics offers beauty as well as insight was first made long ago. Since then, mathematicians have sought to share this discovery and to continue their own search for beauty in mathematics. In recent years, the field of computer graphics has attracted the attention of a number of mathematicians with an eye for beauty. Conducting studies in the complex number system, mathematicians and computer scientists have generated images which are nothing less than spectacular.

This chapter presents a conceptual introduction to the mathematics and art of dynamical systems. This topic is normally studied using computers because of the enormous number of calculations involved. One consequence of this fact is that computer speed and memory resources can make a big difference in day-to-day research activities. For this reason, students considering research projects found in this chapter should plan to use the fastest equipment available. In a practical sense, that means using a Macintosh, an IBM PC, or an IBM-compatible PC rather than an Apple II or a Commodore 64 microcomputer. With that thought in mind, two computer programs written in GW BASIC for IBM-compatible microcomputers are included to get you started.

FUNNY FORMS
AND FRACTALS

Several years ago, the mathematician Benoit Mandelbrot began studying a type of curve that he called a fractal. Fractals have the interesting attribute of being "self-similar"; that is, some feature of the curve is repeated on different scales. One of Mandelbrot's examples of this concept makes use of the coastlines of England, Scotland, and Wales.

When you look at a map of the British Isles, the coastline clearly shows large indentations, or bays. A closer

FROM AFAR,
COASTLINES
OFTEN APPEAR
RATHER SMOOTH.

CLOSE UP,
MANY COAST-
LINES ARE
JAGGED.

look, however, reveals that there are smaller indentations in the shoreline of the large bays. These smaller indentations are, in fact, smaller bays. Bays within bays. Small forms that are repeated on a larger scale. This is the intuitive notion of self-similarity.

Project 87

Other forms in nature exhibit the attribute of self-similarity. Take photographs of these forms and present them as an exhibit of fractals in nature. For instance, if you examine the outlines of puffy clouds, you may recognize fractal forms. Are you interested in rocks and minerals? Go to a rock shop and ask to see some moss agate. The branching forms visible in the moss agate are fractals. Look for variety. Fractals are everywhere!

DYNAMICAL SYSTEMS

In addition to discovering fractals in nature, you can create them yourself. A self-similar array of triangles can be seen in Figure 17. To create the figure, three corner points were plotted for the vertices of a large triangle. A fourth point was then selected at random outside the triangular area defined by the three corner points. (It can be seen to the left of and slightly below the top corner of the large triangle.)

Having selected the three vertices and a fourth point as a "current" point, the following procedure was repeated several hundred times:

Step 1   Randomly select one of the three vertices.

THIS FRACTAL IMAGE SEEMS TO
HAVE A "COASTLINE" OF ITS OWN.

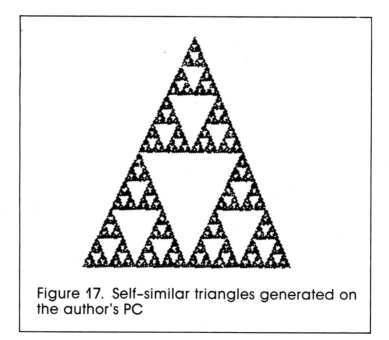

Figure 17. Self-similar triangles generated on the author's PC

Step 2   Plot the midpoint of an invisible line seg-
         ment joining the "current" point and the
         selected vertex.
Step 3   Make the point just plotted the new "cur-
         rent" point.
Step 4   Repeat Steps 1 through 4.

This process of repeating the same operation over and
over is called iteration.

As a second example of iteration, consider the following process using real numbers and the square root
operation:

Step 1   Taking your calculator in hand, enter the
         number 2.

Step 2   Push the square root key.
Step 3   Repeat steps 2 and 3.

In both the midpoint example and the square root example, you are dealing with a dynamical system. Dynamical systems repeat the same operation over and over, each time using the result of the previous calculation as the starting point for the next calculation. The goal is to find out what happens to the calculated values in the long run. In the case of the square root example, it is obvious that the sequence of calculations gets closer and closer to 1. In case of Figure 17, it is far from obvious why the random plotting of midpoints produces such a self-similar figure.

Project 88
Investigate the dynamical system used to produce Figure 17. Attempt to discover why such an interesting pattern is produced.

Project 89
Write a BASIC program which will create Figure 17. Modify the program so you can start with any number of vertices or initial points, plot points other than midpoints, etc. Investigate whether any of these other procedures produce self-similar figures.

Project 90
Investigate a number of dynamical systems of the real number system using familiar operations such as cube root, $1/x$, x^2, $\sin(x)$, etc. Write BASIC programs to do the calculations for you. Include investigations of trigonometric and exponential functions.

Clearly, there are many interesting possibilities for dynamical systems using the real numbers and the real

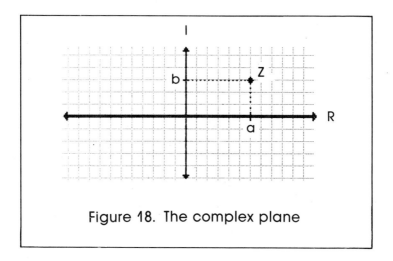

Figure 18. The complex plane

number plane. Some of these dynamical systems produce fractals. However, some of the most interesting fractals are created using the complex number plane.

THE COMPLEX PLANE

The complex plane, as illustated in Figure 18, is represented with its real axis horizontal and its imaginary axis vertical. Using this reference system, any point Z in the complex plane can be represented using an ordered pair (a,b) or as a composite number of the form $a + bi$, where a and b are real numbers and the symbol i is the "imaginary" number $\sqrt{-1}$. Your mathematics teacher can give you an introduction to this number system if you haven't already encountered it in Algebra II or some other math class. Ask your teacher how to add, subtract, multiply, and take roots of complex numbers.

Project 91
Write a set of BASIC programs to do complex arithmetic and root-finding.

DYNAMICAL SYSTEMS OF
THE COMPLEX PLANE

Once you know how to add, subtract, multiply, and find square roots of complex numbers, you are ready to investigate iterative processes with complex numbers.

Define a new dynamical system as follows:

Step 1   Pick any complex number and call it Z.
Step 2   Square Z.
Step 3   Add a constant complex number C.
Step 4   Call this number Z.
Step 5   Repeat steps 2 through 5.

For example,

Step 1   Let $Z = 1 + 1i$ (This is a point outside the
            unit circle centered at the origin.)
Step 2 $Z^2 = (1 + 1i) \cdot (1 + 1i) = 0 + 2i$
Step 3   Let $C = 0 + 0i$, then $Z^2 + C = 0 + 2i$
Step 4 $Z = 0 + 2i$
Step 4 $Z = -4 + 0i$
Step 4 $Z = 16 + 0i$
Step 4 $Z = 256 + 0i$ etc.

This example seems to be headed for infinity along the positive real axis, as indeed it is. Both types of behavior, converging to some number (as in the square root example) or going to infinity are called "normal" behavior in a dynamical system.

Project 92
Write a BASIC program to do the calculations for dynamical systems in the complex number system. If you have written the programs suggested in Project 88, use them as subroutines in this program. Investigate a variety of polynomial, exponential, and trigonometric functions.

REPELLING POINTS

Using the dynamical system based on iterations of Z^2 once again, iterate the first few terms in the sequence which begins with $0.6 + 0.8i$, a point on the unit circle with center at the origin. The first few points are (to five decimal places):

$$
\begin{aligned}
0.60000 &+ 0.80000i \\
-0.28000 &+ 0.96000i \\
-0.84320 &+ -0.53760i \\
0.42197 &+ 0.90661i \\
-0.64388 &+ 0.76513i \\
&\text{etc.}
\end{aligned}
$$

The interesting thing about this sequence is that it does not converge to any number nor does it go to infinity. Every new point in the sequence is just another point on the unit circle. (Try using the Pythagorean theorem to verify this.) In other words, iterating the operation moves the current point around the circle in a chaotic manner, but never generates a point off the circle.

The set of points on this unit circle is called the "repelling set" of the dynamical system. This term derives from the behavior under iteration of points in the vicinity of the repelling set, not from the chaotic behavior of the points in the repelling set itself. If your starting point for the dynamical system is near a repelling point, the set of points produced by the dynamical system moves farther and farther from the repelling point with each iteration. The complete set of all repelling points of a dynamical system is called the system's Julia set. So, for this example, the Julia set is a circle of radius 1 centered at the origin.

MODELING CONCEPTS
WITH A MICROCOMPUTER

The concepts presented above can be illustrated quite easily using a microcomputer and the BASIC programming language. The following program written in GW BASIC (for IBM-compatible microcomputers) systematically iterates the expression $Z^2 + C$ at regularly spaced points in the complex plane, printing the coordinates of the starting point for each set of iterations in the upper-left corner of the screen.

A line is plotted between successive points in the sequence of iterations. As the program runs, you will see lines leave the screen on the way to infinity. You will also see sequences of lines converging to various fixed-point attractors, depending on your choice of C. Occasionally, you may see the chaotic behavior of a point in the Julia set.

```
10 REM GW BASIC FOR IBM-COMPATIBLE
      MICROCOMPUTERS
20 REM DISPLAYS SUCCESSIVE ITERATIONS OF A POINT
30 SCREEN 1
40 REM ENTER THE POINT C = A + BI
50 INPUT "ENTER THE COORDINATES OF THE POINT C "; A,B
60 REM STEP THROUGH THE PLANE SYSTEMATICALLY, 5
      PIXELS PER STEP
70 FOR J = 60 TO 195 STEP 5
80 FOR I = 10 TO 190 STEP 5
90 REM PLOT POINT C
100 PSET (A*100+160,100-100*B)
110 REM CONVERT THE PIXEL LOCATIONS TO COMPLEX
      NUMBERS
120 XX = (J - 160)/100
130 YY = (100 - I)/100
140 REM PRINT THE COORDINATES OF THE STARTING POINT
150 PRINT XX,YY
160 REM START ITERATING
170 FOR C = 1 TO 25
180 REM FIND THE NEXT POINT IN THE SEQUENCE OF
      ITERATIONS
190 X = XX^2 - YY^2 + A
200 Y = 2 * XX * YY + B
```

```
210 REM CHECK ITS DISTANCE FROM THE ATTRACTING
    POINT
220 REM IF THE DISTANCE IS > 2, MOVE TO THE NEXT
    STARTING POINT
230 IF SQR((X − A)^2 + (Y − B)^2) > 2 THEN CLS :
    GOTO 320
240 REM IF THE DISTANCE IS < 2, CONNECT THE
    PREVIOUS POINT
250 REM TO THE NEW POINT WITH A LINE
260 LINE (XX*100+160, 100−100*YY) − (X*100+160,
    100−100*Y)
270 XX = X
280 YY = Y
290 NEXT C
300 REM COMPLETED CHECKING PRESENT POINT, MOVE ON
310 CLS
320 NEXT I
330 NEXT J
```

Apple II users must make the following changes in the program listing:

```
30 HCOLOR = 3 : HGR
70 FOR J = 80 TO 180 STEP 5
80 FOR I = 30 TO 120 STEP 5
100 HPLOT A*50+130, 75−B*50
120 XX = (J − 130)/50
130 YY = (75 − I)/50
230 IF SQR((X − A)^2 + (Y − B)^2) > 2 THEN HGR :
    GOTO 320
260 HPLOT XX*50+130,75−YY*50 TO X*50+130,75−Y*50
310 HGR
```

In both versions of this program, certain choices of C can result in an error message during the program run as the program attempts to plot points off the edge of the screen. If this happens, restart the program using a C closer to the origin of the complex plane, $0 + 0i$.

Project 93

Run the program several times varying the value of C. Observe the location of points which converge under iteration to a fixed point or set of points. Such points often lie in a particular region of the complex plane. Write a BASIC program to plot the region (called the basin of attraction) one point at a time.

JULIA SETS THE EASY WAY

In the case of the dynamical system based on iterations of Z^2, the basin of attraction for the fixed-point attractor at $0 + 0i$ is the interior of the unit circle centered at the origin. The Julia set for Z^2 is the unit circle itself surrounding the basin of attraction. This is an example of a connected Julia set.

Clearly, the Julia set is an interesting feature of any function. But plotting the points of the Julia set need not be approached in the same brute-force manner as the plotting of points in the basin of attraction. The speediest method for finding the Julia set (the set of *repellers*) is based on the notion of an inverse (or reverse) operation.

Each point in the complex plane not in the Julia set is repelled by the Julia set; that is, successive iterations of the function produce points farther away from the Julia set. Since $M(Z) = Z^2$ produces points which recede from the Julia set, the inverse of $M(Z) = Z^2$ should reverse the process, making the Julia set an "attractor." It does.

The inverse of $M(Z) = Z^2 + C$ can be written as follows:

$$Z = \pm \sqrt{M(Z) - C}$$

The following program written in GW BASIC uses this approach to plot the Julia set of functions of the form $M(Z) = Z^2 + C$. Since any point not in the Julia set will converge to some point in the Julia set under inverse iteration, you may enter any point in the plane as a starting point. Your choice of C will determine the particular function under study and its Julia set.

```
10 REM GW BASIC FOR IBM COMPATIBLE
     MICROCOMPUTERS
20 REM PLOTS JULIA SETS OF Z^2 + C
30 CLS
40 SCREEN 1
50 REM ENTER THE COORDINATES OF THE POINT C = A + BI
60 INPUT "ENTER THE COORDINATES OF THE POINT C ";
     CX,CY
70 REM ENTER THE COORDINATES OF A STARTING POINT
80 INPUT "ENTER A STARTING POINT "; WX,WY
90 CLS
100 A = WX − CX : B = WY − CY
110 REM CALL SUBROUTINE TO FIND INVERSE FUNCTION
120 GOSUB 270
130 REM TO AVOID PLOTTING THE INVERSES OF POINTS
140 REM WHICH LEAD BACK TO THE JULIA SET BUT ARE
     NOT PART OF
150 REM THE JULIA SET, THE FIRST FEW INVERSE IMAGES
     ARE "THROWN AWAY"
160 IF N < 10 GOTO 230
170 REM BOTH INVERSE IMAGES ARE PLOTTED
180 FOR P = 0 TO 1
190 PSET (160+A(P)*80,100−70*B(P))
200 NEXT P
210 REM ONE OF THE POINTS IS SELECTED FOR FURTHER
     ITERATION
220 V = INT (2 * RND(1))
230 WX = A(V) : WY = B(V)
240 N = N + 1
250 GOTO 100
260 REM SUBROUTINE TO FIND INVERSES
270 R = SQR(A^2 + B^2) : REM MODULUS OF THE POINT
     UNDER ITERATION
```

```
280 R = SQR(R) : REM MODULUS OF ITS PRE-IMAGE
290 PI = 3.141592654
300 IF A < 0 then TA = PI
310 IF A> 0 THEN IF B < 0 THEN TA = 2 * PI
320 IF A = 0 THEN IF B > 0 THEN T = PI/2 : GOTO 350
330 IF A = 0 THEN IF B < 0 THEN T = 3 * PI/2 : GOTO 350
340 T = ATN(B/A)
350 T = T + TA
360 REM DETERMINE BOTH PRE-IMAGES
370 FOR P = 0 TO 1
380 A(P) = R * COS((T + (P) * 2 * PI)/2)
390 B(P) = R * SIN((T + (P) * 2 * PI)/2)
400 NEXT P
410 TA = 0
420 RETURN
```

Apple II users must make the following changes in the program listing:

```
30 HCOLOR = 3
40 HGR
190 HPLOT 130+A(P)*50,75−B(P)*50
```

Project 94
Investigate the Julia sets of a variety of functions using this program. Look for similarities and differences arising from different choices of C.

Julia sets generated using this program will rarely produce accurate graphics for runs lasting only a few minutes (and possibly regardless of how long the program is allowed to run). It is a feature of many Julia sets that certain points are "visited" *very* rarely during the inverse iteration process. This feature will result in "gaps" in the graphic display. Also, although each inverse function produces two **pre-images** (both of which are plotted), only one of those pre-images is selected for the next

A FRACTAL IMAGE. COMPARE WITH THE
FERN FIDDLEHEADS IN CHAPTER 4.

inverse iteration. This automatically leaves out vast numbers of points in the graphic display. Nevertheless, this program can provide important insights and interesting graphics.

Several Julia sets generated this way are shown in Figures 19, 20, 21, and 22. Table 7 identifies the functions used to generate the figures.

Table 7
Mappings Used to
Generate Figures 19–22

Figure	Mapping
19	Z^2
20	$Z^2 - 0.3$
21	$Z^2 + 0.3$
22	$Z^2 - 1.0$

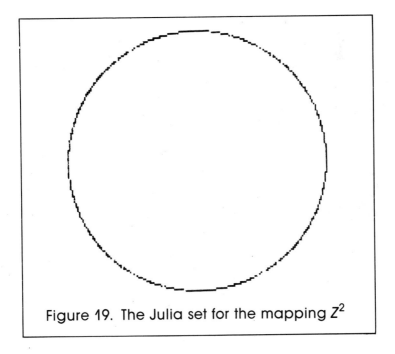

Figure 19. The Julia set for the mapping Z^2

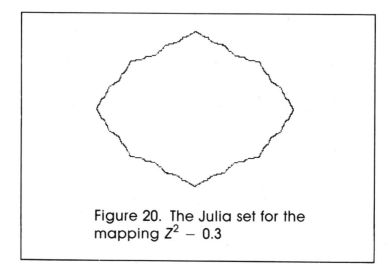

Figure 20. The Julia set for the mapping $Z^2 - 0.3$

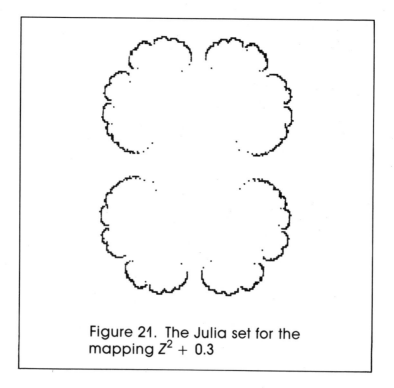

Figure 21. The Julia set for the mapping $Z^2 + 0.3$

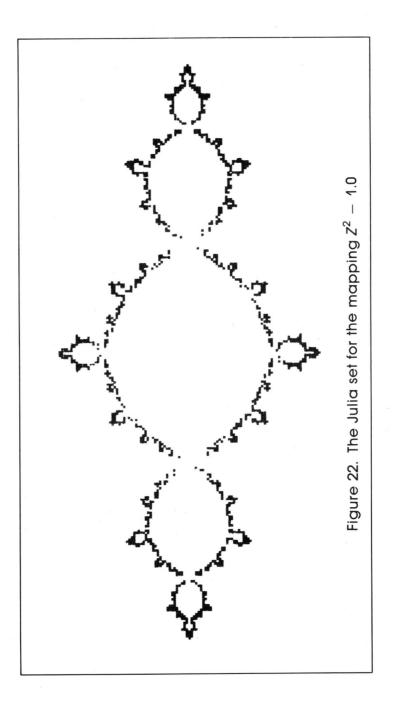

Figure 22. The Julia set for the mapping $Z^2 - 1.0$

THE MANDELBROT SET
AND FRACTALS

After looking at a number of Julia sets, each generated with a different C and the function $Z^2 + C$, it becomes apparent that some Julia sets are connected and some are not. Given such an observation, it is natural to ponder the set of points C for which the function $Z^2 + C$ produces a connected Julia set. Put another way, where are all the points C which produce connected Julia sets?

The set of points which is the answer to this question is called the Mandelbrot set and is one of the most complicated objects in mathematics. The Mandelbrot set is displayed in Figure 23 as the white "budding" or "flaming" object in the picture.

The easiest way to recognize a fractal is to look for self-similarity, that is, the repetition on different scales (sizes) of a particular pattern of line segments. Most Julia sets are fractals. Figure 22 shows this property quite clearly, repeating at smaller and smaller scales the theme of a crown-shaped "bud."

The boundary of the Mandelbrot set is also a fractal. Indeed, not only do the "buds," or "flames," of the Mandelbrot set repeat in varying sizes and locations, but the entire body of the set is repeated infinitely many times! In Figure 23, along the real axis near the left edge of the picture, a small white cross can be seen. If this area is enlarged, it is seen to be a miniature version of the white Mandelbrot set seen in Figure 23. What's more, there are infinitely many such miniatures, all connected to one another.

This is a staggering thought and invites personal investigation. Fortunately, there is a public domain package available to provide just such an opportunity. The collection of programs is called MANDELBROT COLORAMA (TriMark Engineering, 12402 W. Kingsgate Dr., Knoxville, TN 37922) and runs on IBM PC, XT, AT, or compatible computers with 256K or more memory and a

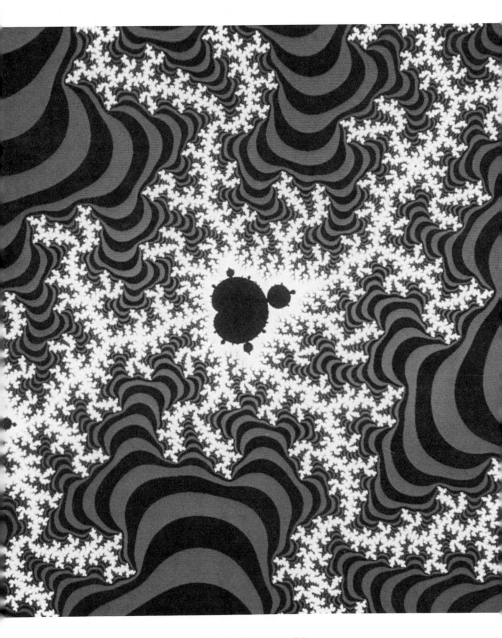

ORDER AND CHAOS
IN THE MANDELBROT SET

Figure 23. The Mandelbrot set

color graphics or compatible adapter. For truly spectacular results, a color monitor may be used.

Figure 24 is a screen dump of the Mandelbrot set
obtained using the SUPERMAN program (the main program). Using cursor controls, a user may define a "window" (portion) of the original set, then "enlarge" that
window to full screen size. This procedure is time-consuming, varying from one to eight or more hours depending
on the location of the window in the original set.

For those looking for quicker images, the program
publisher offers a $15 upgrade (not public domain) which
includes an 8087 version (math coprocessor required)
and the original Pascal source code for the program. The
program publisher claims that this version generates
images in about fifteen minutes.

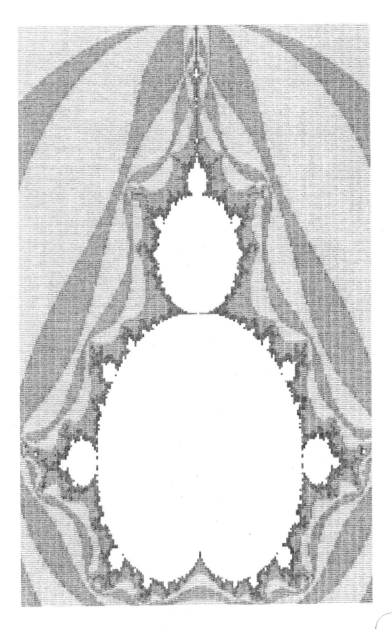

Figure 24. Mandelbrot set generated using the MANDELBROT COLORAMA program

Art Matrix (P.O. Box 880, Ithaca, NY 14851) also offers a computer program for generating fractal images and Julia sets and sells slides and postcards showing fractals and Julia sets.

Project 95
Investigate different regions of the complex plane in the vicinity of the Mandelbrot set using the MANDELBROT COLORAMA program.

Project 96
Select one location of the plane and generate a series of "blowups" of the location using the MANDELBROT COLORAMA program.

GLOSSARY

Arithmetic sequence. A sequence with a constant difference between adjacent terms.

Combinatorics. A branch of mathematics concerned with determining the number of possible outcomes of a given process or the number of possible combinations of a given set of objects.

Conjecture. An informed guess or speculation.

Converge. With respect to an infinite series or sequence, to approach some value as a limit.

Dynamical system. The set of pre-images and images created by an iterated function.

Fibonacci sequence. 1, 1, 2, 3, 5, 8, 13, . . . etc.

Hamilton line. A circuit of a network which passes through each point exactly once.

Heuristics. General problem-solving strategies.

Image. The number generated by a function.

Infinite series. An indicated sum having an infinite number of terms, or addends. For example, $1 + 2 + 3 + \ldots$

Iteration. A process in which the output of one operation serves as the input of the next repetition of the operation.

Lucas sequence. 1, 3, 4, 7, 11, 18, 29, . . . etc.

Mathematical induction. A method of proving certain types of theorems.

Network. A graph using lines to join separate points.

Palindrome. Sequence of characters that reads the same right to left or left to right.

Partition. To divide into parts.

Perfect number. An integer equal to the sum of all of its divisors, other than itself.

Phi, or ϕ. The golden ratio, 1.618033988. . .

Pre-image. The number operated on by a function.

Prime number. A number evenly divisible only by itself and 1.

Probability. A branch of mathematics concerned with determining the likelihood of the occurrence of some event or set of events.

Sequence. A list of terms or objects.

Sequence of partial sums. A sequence, each term of which is the sum of a finite number of terms of a given series.

Series. An indicated sum of terms. For example, 1 + 2 + 3.

Superprime. A prime number which has the additional feature that deleting any number of rightmost digits always leaves a prime.

System of numeration. Counting system, or base.

Tessellation. Interlocking figures leaving no space between.

Theorem. A mathematical rule or law.

Traversable. With respect to a network, a circuit passing through all the points and traversing (following along) each line exactly once.

Triangular numbers. Numbers belonging to the sequence 1, 3, 6, 10, 15, . . . etc.

INDEX

ABOUT THE AUTHOR

Dr. David A. Thomas is a member of the faculty of the Department of Mathematical Sciences at Montana State University. He lives with his wife and daughter in Bozeman, Montana. His favorite pastimes include water-color painting, biking, hiking, and cross-country skiing.